THERE HAS TO BE MORE

RACHEL SERVICE

PRAISE FOR *THERE HAS TO BE MORE*

'I can't think of a single person who would not benefit from this inspiring, heartfelt and practical read. Rachel is the real deal. She's lived and thrived through every lesson in this superbly presented guide to growth. From breakdown to breakthrough, Rachel's personal growth story brings pathos and passion to this clear and proven approach to living your best life. Rachel's approach delivers for her clients again and again. There absolutely is more! Rachel's excellent guide will help you grow into your best life.'

Kylie Walker, CEO, Australian Academy of Technology and Engineering
linkedin.com/in/kylieawalker

'*There Has To Be More* is the kind of resource that helps you define long-term success on your own terms. Rachel is someone who has put the work in to shake off the 'blah' feeling and set herself up for long-term success, all on her own terms.'

Lara McPherson, Founder Rogers Land
rogerslane.net

'If you've been feeling like there has to be more to life – there is! And Rachel guides you on how to get it!'

Phoebe Mwanza, Director, Hueman Equity Consulting
huemanequity.co/phoebe-mwanza

ABOUT THE AUTHOR

Rachel Service, CEO Happiness Concierge™

After experiencing an 'aha' moment at a Beyoncé concert (true story!), with $300 in her bank account, entrepreneur Rachel Service started Happiness Concierge™: the company empowering thousands of people across the globe.

Since then, she has saved companies millions of dollars by empowering their people; partnered with ASX-listed companies, retail banks, universities and government departments; and shifted the dial on workplace culture.

Her award-winning approach to personal and professional growth has been featured in the media and on the TEDx stage, and implemented in companies across the globe.

Rachel's first book, *There Has to Be More: The Essential Guide to Personal Growth* is a summation of her years of frontline experience supporting thousands of individuals to thrive in life and work.

Learn more at rachelservice.com.

First published in 2021 by Major Street Publishing Pty Ltd
PO Box 106, Highett, Vic. 3190
E: info@majorstreet.com.au W: majorstreet.com.au M: +61 421 707 983

A catalogue record for this book is available
from the National Library of Australia

NATIONAL
LIBRARY
OF AUSTRALIA

Printed book: 978-1-922611-10-9
Ebook: 978-1-922611-11-6

Cover design by Tess McCabe
Internal design by Production Works
Printed in Australia by Ovato, an Accredited ISO AS/NZS 14001:2004
Environmental Management System Printer.

10 9 8 7 6 5 4 3 2 1

CONTENTS

CAN YOU RELATE?

'Self-actualization ... the desire to become more and more what one is, to become everything that one is capable of becoming.'
– Abraham Maslow, A Theory of Human Motivation

Years ago, after experiencing anxiety, depression and a break-up, I knew there was just one person who could help me.

Beyoncé.

So, I booked a ticket to see her New York concert.

In New York, as I watched Beyoncé's opening act, tears started to fall. Beyoncé performed for two hours and I sobbed the entire time, crying through every second of 'Single Ladies', 'Halo' and 'Grown Woman'. As I took the subway home and caught my reflection in the window, I saw an exhausted, miserable face. Really, crying at a freaking Beyoncé concert?

If I couldn't enjoy a Beyoncé concert, something had to change. Then and there I realised: *I* was the problem.

Do you ever feel as if you've outgrown parts of your life? Do you feel a bit flat and can't quite put your finger on why? Do you ever secretly wonder, 'Surely there's more to life than this?'

If you ever feel simultaneously overwhelmed and bored by the prospect of continuing with a life that doesn't truly reflect the person you've become, it's likely you've outgrown your life.

Perhaps you've outgrown an element of a relationship. Maybe a job is boring you. Your surroundings might all of a sudden irritate you for no apparent reason. You might simply be going through the motions and feel nothing at all.

In fact, thousands of people I've coached have shared those exact feelings with me, just as I have felt them myself. They explain that they feel trapped by a life they have outgrown and don't know how to get out. They tell me, 'I just feel like there has to be more out there. Surely there's more to life than this?'

That feeling that I had experienced at the Beyoncé concert? It was these feelings exemplified. It's how you feel before you decide to psychologically, emotionally, physically, mentally, professionally or personally make a change. I wasn't breaking (although it felt like it!). I was growing. I knew there had to be more, but I didn't know how to create more.

The wonderful learning is that growth is progression. Growth represents the ability for you to create – or upgrade to – a new reality. To do this, you must get to know yourself, understand how you work and put a structure in place for enjoying life on your own terms.

Thousands of people have felt just like you do. I know I did!

What happened after that Beyoncé concert? I got out my notepad.

I jotted down what I really wanted – not what I thought others wanted, but what I really wanted. I drew a line down the middle of a page and on one side I noted what gave me energy, and on the other I noted which environments, people and jobs depleted my vibe. I started to create a map of myself and how to be my best self – not a 'better' self, but rather someone I could be proud of and excited by every day.

As I uncovered what success looked like to me, I made small changes to my life. I started asking for what I needed. I started saying no to things I didn't want to do anymore. I started making decisions that reflected what I truly wanted. I started wanting, asking for and expecting more.

Growth doesn't need to represent massive changes. It just needs to take you forward in some way. Once I reframed outgrowing my life as a positive, a funny thing started happening. Jobs became more fulfilling. Money started staying in my bank account. Relationships deepened. Instead of fighting with myself, I became more myself. Once I looked at my life and career as something I should strive to outgrow, I started enjoying the present more. I was less obsessed with finding something 'better'; I started to realise that learning was the only constant, and finding joy in continually evolving would take me to where I wanted to go.

Is there really MORE?

Yep! And this book will help you find it.

Within these pages, I share my Growth Cycle for whenever you get stuck. This will help you take safe, sensible, small steps at any stage of your life.

It won't be easy. At times you may want to give up. You might even feel as if you're experiencing an identity crisis at times. But, at its best, this feeling can be the start of something epic.

Since applying these principles to my life, I turned $300 in my bank account into a seven-figure business, became a CEO, got married and did a TEDx talk wearing a hot pink suit. I learned how to say no. I discovered how to get time back. I made more time to spend with those I love. I fell in love again.

The only thing you can control about outgrowing your life is what you choose to do about it. And I'm here to tell you that you have choices, you have power and, with this book, you have a toolkit to make changes that reflect who you've become.

I hope this book shows you that when you have those itchy feelings of 'there has to be more!', instead of feeling frustrated, you'll reach out for the tools in this book and acknowledge that you've outgrown your current life, and you can change it for the future.

It's okay if you feel uncertain or even intimidated by the work you've chosen to do. Millions of people have felt, and do feel, the exact same way.

And for the record, I still cry watching Beyoncé – but now they are tears of pride for how far I have come.

PART 1
HOW DID I END UP HERE?

HOW DID I END UP HERE?

How did I end up here, and what's next?

In this first part of the book, I cover why you may be feeling not quite like yourself, why you're thinking that there has to be more. I encourage you to reflect on what may be causing you to press 'pause' in your life, and review the cost of ignoring your feelings. The truth is that inaction is a choice, and the fact that you're reading this book suggests you have created space to reflect on making changes in line with who you are becoming.

There are several self-reflection sections in the first part of this book. I encourage you to attempt these exercises. At the very least, they will give you pause for thought and open up deeper conversations around what a life on your terms could look like. Many of my clients enjoy doing these exercises solo, and then sharing the insights with a trusted friend, professional coach or counsellor.

Chapter 1

OUTGROWING YOUR OLD LIFE

You may have outgrown one or many parts of your life. Perhaps you've even outgrown yourself.

It is really easy to fall into doing what suits the majority, rather than doing what really makes your heart shine.

We all have a fantasy of rebelling against what other people see as success, but we don't always act due to our fear of what could happen as a result. This is called 'loss aversion'. We are much more motivated by what we could lose instead of what we could gain. This mode of thinking is pretty hardwired into us.

As a result, when it comes to daydreaming about another way to live your life, it is very common to have thoughts of doubt. For example, you might think:

'I could quit my job...' ☺
  '... but where would the money come from?' ☹

'I could get a divorce...' ☺
  '... but what would "so and so" think?' ☹

'I could pivot my career...' ☺
  '... but what would I tell my friends, family or community?' ☹

Breaking up with expectations

What other people think influences so many of our decisions about how we lead our lives. There are implicit and explicit moral and social 'codes' we are expected to follow, depending on where we live and our upbringing. When we behave outside of those codes, we are judged accordingly. Like any decisions that go against the majority, there are consequences to taking action. We are very much products of our environment.

However, breaking up with expectations makes room for your own growth. Taking one small step towards what you need can have such a positive effect. The life you opt into living will be yours, aligned with your view of success, enabling you to get the most out of life – not what someone else expects of you.

It'll take some time to get used to prioritising yourself in a new way at first. However, all the people I have coached over the years go through the exact same cycle. They put themselves out there, commit to growth and, as they evolve, they continue to create an environment that complements who they have become and will become.

A big part of that is re-establishing their relationship with their own expectations, and asking questions such as, 'Is this my version of success or someone else's?' As you go through this process, be open to questioning your own beliefs about success and give yourself permission to rewrite the rules of your life.

Take a moment to reflect on what expectations may be inhibiting a future step, and what an alternative could look like.

Self-reflection

What expectations are you interested in breaking up with?

_____

_____

_____

_____

Who did you learn/absorb these expectations from? What specific moments taught you this?

_____

_____

_____

If you chose to interpret those moments differently, knowing what you know now, what alternative ways could you view those expectations? For example, is it possible you might make different choices, knowing what you know now?

_____

_____

_____

What expectations would you like to create for yourself instead? _(Categories might include: being the first in your family to become an entrepreneur; making it common for someone like you to succeed; or becoming a shining example of what going for what you want looks like!)_

_____

_____

_____

The majority of the people I coach have a real 'aha' moment when they reflect on expectations they've absorbed over the years. It can feel like an emotional release when they say, 'In my family, it's just not expected I…', or, 'Where I grew up, if you did something different to the norm, you were laughed at.' It's quite a moment when you separate yourself from expectation.

The engineer with family expectations

One coaching client I worked with was interested in becoming an entrepreneur to make a difference. When we met, she was working for an engineering firm. There was an expectation she would return home and share her experiences and new-found skills with her community. As the recipient of a scholarship, she felt the added pressure of living up to those expectations.

She was paralysed by family expectations, a fear of not having 'enough' to return home with, and her own desire to expand and grow to create a new venture. It took time to reflect on which elements of those expectations drove her and supported her, and which of those were keeping her from making a positive impact.

We went through an exercise to query how her desire to become an entrepreneur could also support those who loved her. The conclusion she came to was to separate the two. She found that she could take one small step towards fleshing out what her entrepreneurial venture could be and press 'pause' on family expectations until she had a clearer view of what the business looked like, or could look like. This simple step, knowing she could compartmentalise while figuring it out, helped her press 'pause' on the fear that was limiting her ability to take small steps of progress, and create space for creating her new potential reality.

It's so easy to allow unknown fears to creep in and limit our growth. That's why writing expectations down, or sharing them with a trusted counsel, is so powerful.

What stops you from taking action?

For most of us, it's fear.

Fear is ever-present when we try something new. Our brains are simply hardwired to prioritise it.

However, we do forget that fear is a temporary emotion. While it's a helpful tool to alert us to risk, we can choose to either acknowledge it and let it pass, or let it control us and stop us from taking action.

You're not wrong to give fear the time of the day, as fear is there to keep you safe, to let you know uncertainty is on the horizon. Enabling fear to be 'data' to inform your decisions, rather than an emotion that drives your decision-making, is a great first step. You can't let fear drive all the decisions in your life. *Remember: fear is temporary. Regret can last a lifetime.*

Fear manifests itself in many ways. Below I discuss five common fears: fear of judgement, fear of letting others down, fear of leaving your comfort zone, fear of failure and fear of not meeting your own expectations.

Fear of judgement

You might worry what other people will think, or that others will judge you.

The truth is: people are already judging you. Body language experts posit we make assumptions about complete strangers in less than seven seconds. (That's less than the time it takes to say 'hello' in some instances. Yikes!)

The important thing to remember is that how people react to you has little to do with you. What others think or say, most often, is a reflection of how they see themselves. This is referred to as 'projection'.

Projection happens when you 'project' your intention, fears and hopes onto someone else. We all do this from time to time, and most of the time we're not even conscious of it. It's a rare gift to find someone who is actively listening to you without applying their own perspective (which is why you can get so much value out of a coach, therapist or counsellor whose job it is to actively listen without judging).

When you share with others that you'd like to make a change in your life, sometimes the person you're speaking to has a completely unexpected reaction, and this can feel like a judgemental response. It can make you feel dejected.

Just remember, as you go through a process of change, your decisions might seem new or wild to the person hearing about them. You have been thinking about these changes for a while, but for others, your news is, well… news! Instead of being open-minded, others can come across as judgemental and even hurtful. This has nothing to do with you and everything to do with their understanding of how they relate to you. Try to think of this as a short-term price for upgrading your life.

Over time, the right people who are in your corner will understand and support your changes. I'll cover this in more detail in Chapter 9, when I discuss how to chat about your choices with people you love, and what to do if and when they freak out.

Fear of letting others down

When you start questioning elements of your life, you might feel guilty for looking at your life so objectively, especially when it comes to examining your relationships with those you love.

The trap you can fall into when reflecting on your life is worrying about letting others down. This thinking is dangerous, as it implies that someone else's happiness or freedom should come at the expense of your own happiness. But it is more common than you might think.

I find it helpful to remind myself that this mode of thinking lacks logic. How is it fair that you must suffer for others to be happy? You being rich doesn't make someone else poorer. You being fulfilled doesn't make someone else sadder. These things are unrelated. But as we've discussed, we can remember that our desire to fit into others' conventions is a powerful motivator.

So, if you resonate with the idea that you pursuing your next steps may mean letting someone you love down, you might like to do some gentle enquiry with yourself. What do others gain from you staying small or inauthentic to who you're becoming? Are you okay with that, or can you choose to think more of people who love you? You know, they can grow, too.

To counter the idea of letting others down, I'd like to introduce the idea of compromising. Compromising is a part of life and is something that we all do at times. For example, we might stop online shopping to save money, accept someone's quirks to keep the peace or do boring tasks at work for career progression.

But to continue to choose to suffer – when you know better – for someone else's benefit or comfort falls into 'not okay' territory. I understand if safety is a real issue for you, and that opting to keep certain things private is sometimes a matter of life and death. I understand.

However, it's not sustainable. At some point, because you have chosen to compromise, those who love or care about you will ultimately get a compromised version of you. Ironically, they may suffer when they only get half of you.

The corporate escapee turned entrepreneur

I have so many examples of people I've coached and supported who have chosen the long route to what they always wanted. No part of their journey was 'wrong', it simply took some time for them to feel comfortable taking that next step.

In one instance, a client of mine said they'd always wanted to start their own business. They registered the name and the website, and just when it came to actually selling their services, a strange phenomenon started happening. All of a sudden, they'd get offered 'the perfect job'.

This went on for years! They'd find the 'perfect job', find a reason it wasn't perfect, resign and start working on their business. Then, when it came to taking a new step, all of a sudden a new 'perfect job' would pop up!

The perfect reason to not prioritise their dream kept showing up. How odd. Or is it?

No, it's very, very common. Why? The truth is, we create the reality that reflects our fears.

It takes a lot of confidence and courage to make decisions that reflect what we really want, and that can bring up a lot of fears. Instead of reflecting, or taking the time to 'self-coach' and enquire further, we take the shortcut back to that comfort zone, back to what we know. (I know this because I do this all the time before making changes! Life is a step-by-step process.)

In this particular example, the client didn't want to let down people they loved – specifically, their parents. In my client's mind, those people saw success differently. A solid job in a corporate company with a fancy title was success.

And look, anything can look pretty great when the alternative is something new or scary. But behind the fear of putting themselves out there and finding new clients was something much more compelling, which drove their behaviour – the fear of letting those they loved down by 'failing' according to someone else's version of success.

Through deep introspection, this client was able to reframe this fear into a positive. It took some time, but hey, fears don't just go 'poof' and disappear when we want them to. In this client's instance, they needed time to think of themselves as having the identity of being a business owner, and to fortify their sense of safety and belonging around that.

To help them take that step, they surrounded themselves with other like-minded people who also had taken risks in their career. They listened to podcasts. They went to panels and talks. They got coffee with other entrepreneurs! They started to talk with their network about what they wanted to do more of, to 'test the waters'.

By doing so, this 'crazy idea' stopped seeming so at odds with who they were and truly reflected who they were having the confidence to become. They started to feel like themselves again as they talked about their dream business.

It took them years, many years, to take the step into launching their business. Sometimes we have to go backwards before we can go forward, you know? The point is, we always have a choice. With reflection, we can take the fear data, ask if it's true or helpful, and seek support to take positive action. Over time, we can take steps that reflect our hopes and dim those fears.

I also want to note that your decision to change your life is not a criticism of those you love, or those who have supported you earlier in your life. These things are not related, although it certainly might feel like it during a time of change!

Instead, I encourage you to think about how you are simply evaluating how to bring out the best in yourself and live the life you really want. Anyone who is secure in themselves and who wants the best for you will endorse this.

At first, others might find your change a bit scary, too. They might worry about losing you, or mourn the loss of a type of relationship they felt secure in. Try to reassure yourself, and them, that you are reflecting on your life so you can live your best life. You aren't making any decisions for now. The first step is simply reflecting on what lights you up so you can be your best self for yourself and those you love.

Even if you do get pushback, don't give up on reflecting. This is something you can do in the privacy of your own mind for a little while before taking action – and it's free.

Remember, those who love you may look to you as a role model. You have to be brave to show those who love you what it looks like to be healthy and fulfilled. You might find it helpful to remember that when you are at half-mast, they only get half of you. They are not getting you at your best and most rested, rational and kind.

You also might not yet be surrounding yourself with a group of people who have already made that transition. Like our corporate-escapee-turned-entrepreneur, the move felt so 'out there' until they met people who were doing it, and soon it became their 'norm'.

Fear of leaving your comfort zone

Another fear that may stop you from taking action towards growth is the fear of leaving your comfort zone. To overcome this fear, you need to humble your ego with the reality that you will become a 'beginner' of sorts. You'll feel as though you're starting from scratch. It won't feel very comfortable at first! But it's necessary to grow.

Here's an example.

My five-year-old niece and I were throwing paper planes out the window from an upstairs bedroom. Downstairs, her dad was laughing and encouraging her to keep going. Energised by the response, she upgraded from paper planes and threw out... a plate. She threw a plate out of the window.

'Oh darling,' I said in disbelief, 'we don't throw plates out the window.'

She looked up to me. 'Sowwy, Wach. I'm still learning.'

I retold this story to her parents. They laughed. 'Oh yes, they teach her that at kindergarten. If you make a mistake, you apologise and you tell the other person you're still learning the rules.'

My darling niece might not have got it right with the plate incident, but she was pushing herself out of her comfort zone... she was 'still learning'. When we learn, we experience a sense of achievement. And achievement is key in pursuing a life of fulfilment.

According to German educator and adventurer Tom Senninger, there are three 'zones' of learning:

1. **Comfort zone:** Most of your actions and thoughts are habits. When you are in your comfort zone, you're essentially on autopilot, expending the least amount of energy. You don't need to think much or make major decisions day to day. Things feel pretty easy.

2. **Learning zone:** This is where you learn, grow and develop. It's where you are using more brain space to take on more capacity, so it takes more out of you. You might feel on the 'edge' of your competence and, as a result, feel clumsy or awkward during this phase as you are experiencing some things for the first time.

3. **Panic zone:** In this zone, you are in fight, flight or freeze mode (which is what happens when you're under extreme stress). When you operate from a place of panic – even if you enjoy the feeling – your body produces higher levels of the stress hormone cortisol. While this zone can energise some people, over time it depletes your energy as it uses so much adrenaline to keep your body functioning. If you, like me, have ever experienced burnout (adrenal fatigue), exhaustion or overwhelm, this might feel familiar to you and, therefore, comfortable. Just know that as helpful as adrenaline is, it is a high-value resource that needs to be replenished. Take it from someone who has learned this the hard way!

Here are a few fun facts about the panic and comfort zones:

- Incompetence lives in both. And I'm not just talking about incompetence at work. I'm talking about the ability to be present, actively listen to those you love and care about, contribute to meaningful relationships and friendships, look after your health and wellbeing, and grow and develop.

- It can be dangerous to operate from your panic or comfort zones the majority of the time. When you are not actively engaged in what you are doing, you are more likely to make errors and forget important tasks.

- You can also feel as if you are on a high when you are in the panic zone. If you're an adrenaline junkie, this might be quite appealing. When clients come to me for help, they're often in their panic zone and have manifested 'busyness' in almost every area of their life to distract themselves from feelings of dissatisfaction and uncertainty.

But wait... what if my panic zone *is* my comfort zone?

Throughout my twenties and a decent chunk of my thirties, I permanently lived in my panic zone – so much so that it actually felt like my comfort zone. Being really busy was comforting because – applying it to my work – it was intellectually stimulating, and it gave me a deadline (my motivator) and a sense of momentum, accomplishment and what behavioural psychologists call 'mastery'. It gave me a sense of competence, control and self-respect. So, there were plenty of 'pros' in one sense.

On the other hand, our bodies can only handle so much stress! My body ran out of adrenaline, and in some very extreme instances I was unable to stand up, walk, have coherent thoughts and conversations or even organise any area of my life.

Getting to work was one such example. In one instance, my parents stepped in and spoke to my workplace, and I took sick leave while I learned how to be a functioning adult again. I took six months off work and had to be assigned a guardian to ensure I worked part time while building up my strength again. I had made myself sick, and for six months I was unable to figure out how to get to the supermarket to look after my basic needs, let alone create an income for myself. Looking back, it now seems astonishing, but at the time I was so busy ignoring the hunger pains and feelings of busyness that I really didn't notice I was slowly but surely making myself sick.

And let's be real: I achieved a lot during my twenties and thirties. I worked for Academy Award and Grammy Award-winning artists. I interviewed famous people. I travelled the world. I fronted rock bands, country bands and even an Elvis impersonator band at one point! I had a great time. I'm still proud of what I achieved. But since then, I've had to learn to redefine what my comfort zone looks like so it can fuel me, not ruin me.

I needed to figure out a way to not feel so exhausted after every exciting assignment. I needed to learn how to have enough 'petrol in the tank' to continue to evolve and grow, to continue to seek opportunities that led to my goal of achieving mastery and accomplishment. And while I knew intellectually it made sense to prioritise this, for some reason I never did.

I remember complaining to my therapist about it. I was sick and tired of feeling sick and tired! 'I'm not convinced you want to change, Rachel', she said. Gulp. That was enough for me to get out of my own way. I was all talk and no action! I was saying one thing, then doing the same things that got me into those very scenarios I said I wanted to avoid! I wasn't being honest with myself, which only exacerbated my anxiety and feelings of guilt. I had to be the person who made a change, and I had to stop being sick and tired of being sick and tired and actually do something about it.

And so, the humbling process of learning began again. See where I'm going with this? Once you think you know yourself, by growing you are learning, and as such you will feel like a beginner over and over again. As they say, you get the lesson again and again until you've learned it.

The way to experience fulfilment is to step into your learning zone. When you are in your learning zone, you grow.

If you're reading this book, you might have been spending a fair bit of time in your comfort zone. You might have 'moved in' to your zone and not know how to get out.

Knowing where your comfort zone starts and ends can be key to identifying how to learn and grow.

Self-reflection

Analyse the zones you work and live your life in.

What observations do you make about your relationship with your own comfort, learning and panic zones?

_____

_____

_____

_____

_____

_____

Which areas of your comfort zone energise you? *(Examples: being with friends, doing something I'm good at, having fun)*

_____

_____

_____

_____

_____

Which areas of your comfort zone deplete you? *(Examples: certain types of work, obligations, doing something I'm good at but don't enjoy)*

_____

_____

_____

_____

What areas of your life do you think help you stay in your comfort zone? *(Examples: work and a regular salary, friends I grew up with)*

When was the last time you were in your learning zone?

What did you observe about yourself as you reflected on the zones?

Fear of failure

Your definitions of success and failure may be based on others' expectations or versions of success.

When you create failure criteria based on others' expectations, there is no way for you to succeed. This book is all about creating your own definition of what success looks like. You get to define what you expect of yourself. You get to direct this scene! When you act according to your own belief systems, your expectations for yourself and your definition of success, that is your power in action.

Don't give up your power for some vague idea of success. You get to trademark your own version of success.

For now, I want you to consider replacing the idea of 'failure' with either your own definition or by answering this question: 'What would letting myself down look like?'

Let's look at some examples to get you started:

😊 *Success could be finishing one section of this book a month and doing the reflection exercises.*

☹️ *Letting yourself down could be, instead of picking up the book each evening, reverting to your comfort zone to scroll on social media instead!*

😊 *Success could be deciding not to moan about a co-worker anymore.*

☹️ *Letting yourself down could be letting fear stop you from asking yourself what's really bothering you about them.*

😊 *Success could be deciding that making decisions at work based on your values is important to you.*

☹️ *Letting yourself down could be leading with ego instead of integrity.*

☺ *Success could be making a deal with yourself to spend one hour a week writing a blog, just as I did years ago.*
☹ *Letting yourself down could be stopping this practice.*

The point is that *you* get to decide. Only you know what success looks like from your perspective.

Fear of failing to meet your own expectations

Some of my clients are all-or-nothing thinkers. This means that if something doesn't work out as planned, they throw in the towel, give up, get frustrated and rarely pick up the goal again.

To help you manage that process, I invite you to create a range of ways to win by lowering your expectations. I know what you're thinking: 'Didn't you say to create my own expectations? And now you want me to lower them?!'

Well... yes, I did, but bear with me. I am not asking you to lower your standards. I am asking you to lower your expectations to create the room for you to succeed.

'You know, Rachel,' a therapist once told me, 'you'd have a much better time if you lowered your expectations.'

Um, excuse me? Lower my expectations? Are you mad? 'If you lower your expectations, you'll put less pressure on yourself and others, and as a result, you'll enjoy yourself more,' she said.

It turns out, my high expectations of myself were stopping me from noticing the wonderful things already going on in my life.

The advice I now give others (including my own team) is, when starting something new that you have never done before, triple the amount of time you think it's going to take. Then cut your expectations of what 'good' looks like in half. Trust me,

I'm setting you up for success here by helping you experience small wins to keep your momentum going.

If you have never done something before, you are unlikely to be exceptional at it. That's not a reflection of your competence or skill level. It's simply what my experience of working with thousands of people has shown me. Having the discipline to keep trying, even if you don't like what the first go produces, is what showing yourself respect looks like. Respect yourself enough to be kind to the person you're about to become as you step into your learning zone for a little while.

Failing is not a full stop. It's a chance for you to reflect and ask yourself what stopped you or enabled your fear of failure. Then you can adjust the steps that are going to work for you.

Results don't exist in a vacuum. Give yourself some grace by thinking flexibly, not in absolutes. With fewer 'rules', you'll have more space to succeed.

Positive thinking isn't just for self-help gurus

Overriding your fear of what you might lose by reframing it in terms of what you could gain is a process experts call 'anxiety appraisal'. This is the process of utilising excitement – which is a similar emotion to anxiety in that it is a state of arousal – to change your mindset to one of 'opportunity' rather than 'threat'. In a Harvard Business School study, participants who reappraised anxiety as excitement performed 22 per cent better at maths tests; they were 17 per cent more persuasive when public speaking and even sang 17 per cent better. Instead of focusing on what they could lose, or what could go wrong, participants were asked to focus on what they could gain, and they performed better as a result. This is a great way to prepare for your growth process. When thoughts of 'what could go wrong' crop up, acknowledge them, then ask: 'If that is the case, what could go right? If I choose to act, what could I gain?'

As you step out of your comfort zone, you will make mistakes. You'll be clumsy with your words. You'll fumble and fall, say the wrong thing, do stupid stuff. You'll do embarrassing things and wonder what you were thinking. You don't know what you don't know, after all. But failure, well, that is up to you.

You get to define success, and failure is completely on your terms. It's your definition that matters, no one else's. A big part of this book will, I hope, remind you that you can – and need to – change the narrative if you want your dream to work. You need to step into your power.

Your only liability is giving airtime to fears instead of taking action.

To do this, don't let someone else's idea of success become your goal. Your goal is to create your own.

Chapter 2

THE REAL COST OF AVOIDING YOUR FEELINGS

Happy doesn't just 'happen'. All elements of your life impact your experience.

The major consequence of not trusting how you feel is that you live in opposition to your true self.

Being miserable makes you self-focused and, yes, inherently selfish. It's also why unhappiness can be very isolating and dangerous. It shuts you off from your network. You can feel lonely, despite plenty of people surrounding you and trying to help. It's impossible to give to others, to offer joy, to share your life's work with passion and authenticity when you feel unfulfilled inside (unless you're authentically miserable, that is). Feeling miserable sucks energy out of you and those who love you. In all my experiences before my burnouts, there was a little voice in my head saying, 'Something doesn't feel right.' I ignored it. The consequence was concern and unhappiness for everyone involved. I wasn't the only one who was affected by the drama: my friends, family and partners were all affected by picking up the pieces of someone they cared for.

My story is a cautionary tale, but one that ended well. I discovered I was the problem at that Beyoncé concert, but what I didn't know yet was that I could also be the answer.

As I said earlier, to grow, you must stop compromising and take action. You must make different choices. There will always be a cost to change. By focusing on what your own non-negotiables are, you pave the way to let go of what no longer serves you.

Don't wait until you can't enjoy things like you used to. Instead, tell yourself there is another feeling on the other side of fear, of action, and it is growth. It is hard, it is work, but it is absolutely worth it.

To help you mentally untie yourself from scenarios that no longer support who you are or who you are becoming, I invite you to create a checklist of things you are okay with walking away from, to make room for the things you will walk towards. Over time this list will evolve, just as you do.

Write down any words, environments, dynamics, behaviours or scenarios that no longer serve you. After you have outlined what you are no longer interested in endorsing, take some time to reflect on what you are interested in moving towards. This can be as vague as a feeling or as specific as a goal; it's really up to you. It's a helpful reflection tool to use throughout your life and with those you love.

To help you with this self-reflection, here are some examples of what some of my clients chose to move away from:

- complaining about a situation they had the power to change
- a mindset in which they told themselves they shouldn't expect or deserve more

- relationships that focused on the negatives instead of the positives
- jobs that they knew they could do, so they didn't fail.

And instead, they chose to make room to move towards becoming someone who:

- instead of participating in gossip, chooses to walk away from it
- instead of accepting others' definitions of success, chooses to believe they can have more
- instead of accepting relationships where they are undermined, chooses to participate in dynamics where they are respected – as the minimum!
- instead of saying yes to everything, shares their boundaries and says no
- instead of shying away from communicating their needs, starts to feel comfortable being assertive
- instead of downplaying their interests, gives themselves permission to think about how they might transfer their skills to roles that reflect their current interests.

You can have control over your life; you just have to be brave and take it. Making choices that serve you and taking the lead in your own life can start now. I promise you, it's worth it.

Self-reflection

I am moving away from…

People who _____

_____

_____

_____

_____

The mindset that _____

_____

_____

_____

_____

Environments that _____

_____

_____

_____

_____

People who do/think _____

_____

_____

_____

A dynamic where _____

_____

_____

_____

To make room to move towards…

People who _____

_____

_____

_____

_____

The mindset that _____

_____

_____

_____

_____

Positive environments that _____

_____

_____

_____

_____

People who do/think _____

_____

_____

_____

_____

A dynamic where _____

_____

_____

_____

Inaction is a choice

Action is the tool to use to move from your comfort zone to your learning zone. It is the most effective path to change.

One effect of inaction is that it zaps your confidence. By not taking action, you give your power away. You send yourself the message that you can't take charge of your life, and that is absolutely not true.

Another impact of inaction is the likelihood of overanalysis and, therefore, a sub-par result. In a study of gamblers, it was found that those who revised their initial bet generally delivered a worse performance. Why? Researchers said they 'should have stuck with their initial judgments, or their "gut instincts"'. Our gut is powerful and knows more than we often give it credit for.

The vagus nerve is an element of our parasympathetic nervous system, which is responsible for a range of bodily functions including mood regulation, digestion and heart rate. The nerve also connects the gut and brain, sending messages in both directions; this is called the gut-brain axis. So, when something 'doesn't feel quite right', or 'your gut' is giving you information, you can blame it on your vagus nerve.

If you have strong feelings in your gut, you might also at times mistake fear of action for a real threat. It will certainly feel like it! Remember, as a species, we make the majority of our decisions to avoid fear and pain.

So, as you consider an action, you might experience your body telling you, 'Don't do it! Put it off a little bit longer! Avoid more feelings like this!'

Inaction can seem appealing in the moment. However, if you want to live life on your own terms, you can no longer give the keys to your behaviour to someone else. You cannot rely on your employer, for example, to have all the answers. You need to take control of the steering wheel of your life.

You can work with the data your gut gives you, gently enquiring as to whether it's a real threat or simply a feeling of uncertainty, as you step towards something new, unknown or not done before (by you). Gently asking, 'Is this information helping me stay small, or is it my gut helping me see I'm doing something new in my learning zone?' can be a great opportunity to reframe. Often, we overlook chances to do incredible things purely because we get scared off by our all-powerful gut. 'It doesn't feel right' is a valid reason to pause. I'm asking you to pause and gently enquire as to whether the message is helpful, keeping you from harm, or your body saying, 'We are going to do something new and I'm scared, but I'm going to take action anyway!'

Both responses are valid, and only you know the answer for your unique situation.

Moving from inaction to action that serves you requires a mindset switch from 'waiting for change' to 'taking control of your life'. By accepting this responsibility, you will find making decisions in your life relatively straightforward. As the saying goes, you can either accept your situation, change your situation or leave your situation. Every choice has consequences, but never forget you always have a choice. Inaction robs everyone of growth.

Companies engage me to help employees maximise their potential. This means I work with managers who are, at times, really concerned about their employees. Some of the scenarios managers have spoken to me about include the following:

- 'Our employee doesn't participate the way they used to. Has something changed?'

- 'Our employee used to be a star performer; now they're a real grump. Did something happen?'
- 'We're worried our employee is going through something privately and are uncertain how to support them.'
- 'Our employee seems to be on autopilot, saying yes to everything. We're worried they're on the train to burnout.'
- 'Our employee has been refusing to participate for a really long time. We don't know what to do about it.'

The commonality all of the above concerns share is that something had indeed changed: their employees had grown and had one foot in the door and one foot out. They all wanted to leave but didn't do anything about it. Instead, they stayed, stuck in their comfort zone, and over time their performance suffered. With my help, some were empowered to leave; others were performance-managed into leaving. The point is, inaction when you are unhappy or not aligned with what you are doing doesn't solely impact your wellbeing: it can affect your career and reputation, and deny other people opportunities to grow.

Don't choose inaction at work

You don't want to be the person people shrug their shoulders at or roll their eyes about. You want to be the star who continues to grow, and has a reputation for doing the right thing and enough integrity to make tough decisions.

If you are not enjoying your comfort zone, if it is bringing you pain and suffering, if you are inflicting your pain and discomfort upon others, you need to step up and do something about it. Your boss will thank you. By removing yourself from a role that is not the right fit, you free your boss to find someone who desperately wants it.

The key lesson here is simply this: you always have a choice. Doing nothing about your situation is a choice. Staying miserable is a choice. Asking for help is a choice. Doing something with that help is a choice.

If you don't yet feel in control of your life, I understand. The good news is that you can choose what you do from here. Awareness is the first step. The next is making a plan; then, taking action. When you make the choice to take control of what you want, you perform differently. You become more confident, competent and effective. The gift of taking small steps towards growth is that when you do, something amazing happens: your confidence grows. When you see yourself as being in control of your life, you make better decisions. You start showing up at work. You match your words with your actions. You stop ignoring what does not make you happy, proud or fulfilled and start making steps to feel better every day. You start to feel proud of yourself, and as a result, your self-confidence and self-esteem grow.

Confidence isn't a personality trait

One big reason our confidence dips during times of change is because we aren't being honest with ourselves. We are saying one thing and doing something completely different. We are acting one way and thinking another.

When clients come into my care, their confidence is shaky, and that's because they feel as though they're having an 'affair' with their thoughts. They're saying 'yes' out loud and are screaming 'no' deep inside!

They feel as though their private self is having a secret life away from their public self, and as a result, they feel guilty. And guilt can show up in insidious, confidence-knocking ways.

The good news is that confidence isn't a personality trait: it's a skill which is a direct reflection of actions we choose to take.

I mean, no one (I sincerely hope) was googling 'when will Rachel Service have an "aha" moment about her burnout and start a business to help other people like her?' I had to do what I'm terrible at on Tinder: I had to make the first move and put myself out there.

You can build up confidence in small incremental steps that reinforce what you want to do more of. Here's a powerful tool to help you do that.

Your Confidence Equation

A practical tool we use at Happiness Concierge is the Confidence Equation, and it can be such a valuable reference when creating a life and career that has more for you. It's really simple:

Confidence = Evidence + Validation + Self-belief.

When you have evidence of a life that reflects your desires, validation that your choices serve you and others in meaningful ways and self-belief that you can have what you desire, you move away from uncertainty and towards action. Whenever you feel your confidence slowing down or lagging, you can come back to the equation and reflect: 'Does my evidence, validation or self-belief need a top-up?'

Let's look at some examples.

Create evidence in your equation by completing an Achievement Audit

We feel confident when we play to our strengths and have examples of our success. The things we find 'easy' are often the things we're naturally skilled at. (Interesting, that!) But because they come easy to us, we're sometimes inclined to think they're less valuable. So, it can be a game changer to document your achievements so that you have cold, hard evidence of being successful to reinforce your competence. I call this completing an 'Achievement Audit', and thousands of my clients have told me how it has given them a huge confidence boost during times of change, or when they feel on the 'edge' of their competence as they develop a new skill or mindset.

Self-reflection

Take a moment to write down and capture your achievements. You can use the start of the week, month, year or decade as a place to start, depending on what is most relevant to you.

What have I achieved this week/month/year/decade?

_____

_____

_____

_____

What was the impact? How did it feel?

_____

_____

_____

What did I learn as a result?

_____

_____

_____

Document meaningful validation from people you admire who respect you

By taking a moment to document meaningful validation of the impact we've contributed to, or the impact our work has perhaps made on others or paved the way ahead for, we can get valuable feedback on the role we play, or have played in the past.

Pro tip: so often we seek validation from people whose perspectives we don't even respect, or from people who don't see our future steps as we do! This is why it can be really disappointing when we receive a deflating piece of feedback.

I'll give you an example. When I was growing Happiness Concierge, I reached out to another entrepreneur. When I ran my plans past them – to expand the team and create an amazing group of talented Happiness Concierge Culture Consultants – to get a bit of validation that it was possible, I was quite shocked when they said, 'Oh Rach, that'll never work. Your clients will always want you and not a team.'

I realise now that they were speaking from their own experience, not mine. So, it took me a few moments to ask myself, 'Hmm… who could I seek validation on this idea from?' I knew in my gut the idea could work, and I really craved stepping it through with someone to get feedback on how to make it a reality. When I went back to my validation list, I had a few other people I could ask to get some feedback from, including my business coach. My coach was able to validate my business model against comparable examples in other markets, and through a short conversation, I'd mapped out my next steps.

The difference between the entrepreneur and the coach? One of them could see my vision.

As you reach out for validation, or cast your mind back to previous feedback, this handy checklist can provide a helpful framing:

- Has this person done what I want to do one day?
- Is this person on my team?
- Is this person capable of hearing me without casting their own doubts, negativity or insecurities?
- Has this person experienced me at my best self?

You can also seek validation from those you work or socialise with. For example, after a great interaction with a client or a friend, you can ask any of these questions:

- 'Reflecting on our work history, what are two things you have found I do well that add value?'
- 'I'd love some feedback on how you've found this process. What has worked well for you?'
- 'As my friend, what would you say are my three top strengths?'

Something that I did before starting Happiness Concierge was to send an email to everyone I knew who supported me and people I didn't know too well but admired. I told them I was looking to do something new, that I didn't know what it was yet but that I'd value their feedback on what they felt my strengths were and what they could see me doing in the future. Here is the email:

Hi there!

As you're someone I admire and respect, I'd love to get some feedback from you. I'm going through a process where I'm reviewing my next steps, and your answers to these questions will help me greatly. I appreciate it!

- What would you say my top two strengths are?
- What would you pay me to do, knowing I could pull it off and you have confidence I'd do a great job?
- What could you see me doing in the future?

The results were so validating. To my delight, most people said they could see me having a TV show one day and they'd pay me to make anything happen. They saw me as unstoppable and determined. I was growing, and even though I didn't know what the precise next steps would be, knowing other people had my back and had faith in me was really empowering.

Creating ways to increase your self-belief

Self-belief is an astonishing thing. It can take you towards your goals, or it can demolish them. It is incredibly important; as you define what having 'more' in your life looks like to you at each life stage, you are creating the space to positively develop your self-belief and a healthy relationship with how you see yourself and what you're capable of.

One reason maintaining self-belief is such an enduring task in our lives is because it is built upon three elements of confidence:

1. Being clear on what we want
2. Believing we have the ability to achieve what we want
3. Believing we deserve what we want.

Typically, when clients of mine have worked on their evidence, sought respectful validation and are still stalled on their goals, it's because one of the above is causing them to pause.

What I have learned is that if you are unclear on what it is you want, you won't take steps towards understanding what a life with 'more' means. If you doubt your ability, you will likely talk yourself out of taking steps towards your goals. And finally, if you do not believe you deserve more, you won't take action.

I find it reassuring to remember this when I find myself pausing on my own goals. Recently, I was working on a revenue goal for my business. For some reason, when it came to doing what was a relatively small task to shift the dial, every day I found almost every reason in the book why I couldn't! I was too 'busy', 'something else came up', or I felt really 'tired'. You name it, I found the perfect excuse not to do it!

Realising this, I had a check-in with myself. I was saying I wanted to increase my revenue, but I wasn't doing a single thing that would increase my chances of this. Why? Through enquiry, I realised I had a clear goal, I knew what I wanted and I knew I had the ability, but to be successful at that new level required a whole new dose of self-belief around what I felt I deserved!

Outdated, unhelpful 'rules' I'd created earlier in my entrepreneurial career were holding me back. I thought I deserved success only if I worked as hard as possible. Some part of me couldn't quite get my head around making money being easy, playing to my strengths, and delivering best-in-class value. Some small part of me thought I needed to suffer more to grow! Honestly, even this author needs to take her own advice!

Through the support of my coach, I was able to unpack this gently and reflect on upgrading my system. I wanted more, and to enable that, I had to consciously work on feeling I deserved success. Through reframing work as input, I started to look at the combined value of what I had spent years making, and instead of thinking 'time = money', I started to see 'value = revenue'.

As you read this, you might wonder, 'How will I know which element will help me take a step forward?' To answer that, here are questions that can guide your experience:

- If I were to start having an honest conversation with myself, what would I discover that I want, truly?
  (In Chapter 6, you will find creating your 'I Want' Lists a valuable exercise to extrapolate what this looks like for you.)
- If I had the ability to achieve it, what would having 'more' in my life and career look like?
- Is it true I lack the ability? Or do I lack confidence?
- If I were to be successful in getting more of what I wanted, what would that mean? Would I still be loved? Accepted? Valued?

Be gentle with yourself as you reflect on these questions, and know you can always come back to them if and when you experience roadblocks in your growth evolution.

Tips to cultivate validation and evidence at work

I have spent years wondering whether my work had an impact, and I went to huge degrees to create value. As you know, I burned out many times, and I now know that not having that feedback loop of what was adding value versus what was 'busy work' played a role in this.

At Happiness Concierge, I've built an evidence and validation system into our ways of working. At the close of each assignment, each participant is invited to provide feedback on their experience, including what specifically enabled them to take positive action and one piece of advice they'd have for the team if they were to have the experience again.

Complementing this step is a process where I personally touch base with every client to understand what helped them shift the dial, and I ask for one piece of feedback on what was unique or special about their experience. I invite one-on-one feedback on their experience.

I then document this in our web form, called 'Kudos'. This generates an email, which gets sent to me and I then forward to the relevant team member, and which is saved on a central database. From this, I can personalise my thanks of the comment and let this person know that I've seen it, which is great for visibility as the company continues to grow. The team also has access to the Kudos web page, meaning they can share their great feedback with peers, too. My team members tell me they love saving these emails and referring to those evidence and validation points when they need a confidence boost!

When the time comes to complete the project review, discuss a performance review or celebrate the end of a successful quarter, the team and I reference these tangible pieces of evidence to share and reinforce what is working well, as well as getting data on how to improve our experience for clients and those in our care.

Some of them have even shared that they read their Kudos emails as a digital pep talk before saying yes to an exciting assignment or going into a new client meeting. When I first started Happiness Concierge, I wanted to create an environment where anyone could leave an interaction with us and say to someone who loved them, 'See what I did?' and beam with pride. Celebrating accomplishments feels even better when you can share them.

It's also not all about you

Moments of limbo have flow-on effects for everyone around you: your family, colleagues, friends and dependants. They all pick up on how you're feeling and take cues from it.

Although how we feel is not biologically contagious, there is evidence to suggest it influences how others interpret our intentions, how they respond to us, how likely they are to take us seriously and how much they meet our energy levels. As you read this book, I would like to invite you to start a serious conversation with yourself: to allocate time to get clear on your goals so you can focus your energy, and to take real steps towards actualising those goals so you can better serve those in your care as a walking, talking example of what is possible.

Bad things happen when you become complacent. Don't let complacency take control of your life.

It's time to make a change

If you feel, as I certainly have, that there's a disparity between your private and public self, that you're spreading yourself thin because you're being lots of different versions of yourself for others, and that you are mentally and emotionally disintegrating to make others feel more comfortable, well, guess what? You'll end up paying some form of price: be it opportunity cost (because you're busy doing stuff that doesn't actually serve you), financial cost (because you're only earning as much as your perceived worth, and that influences how you see yourself), cost to your emotional and mental stability, an eroded confidence over time, or in some cases your physical safety, or even burnout from just being really bored.

Psychologist Jeremy Sherman writes, 'The instinct to survive is strong. The instinct to alleviate fear is stronger.'

Surely, being 'ourselves' doesn't have to be work, does it? Well, it kind of does.

However, the great thing about making a change is you start to take control. And that brings confidence, which gets stronger the more you put in the tank, the more you hang out with your people who reinforce you're not alone, and remind you that there are other people out there who think and act like you do. Tiny acts will have a snowball effect on your confidence and how you see yourself, and will directly influence what you're able to achieve. They will positively impact every factor of your life.

You are not throwing away everything that has served you to date. Rather, you are respecting those things enough to thank them for their presence and taking the next step forward.

You are not the only benefactor of making decisions that suit you. Your offspring, niblings, friends, family and colleagues all hear your intent loud and clear: 'If I can take myself seriously, so can you.'

You mustn't make decisions based on what you can lose. Instead, you must approach them with what you have to gain.

Self-reflection

Think about your private and public selves.

In what ways do you deny your 'private self' (what you really think) airtime?

What specifically do you worry about people saying?

Are these specific people who know you as a certain person? (List them here.)

What does their perspective/feedback mean about their world view?

How aligned are you with that world view?

_____

_____

_____

_____

How do your current actions endorse that world view?

_____

_____

_____

_____

In what ways will continuing to make decisions based on appeasing that judgement stop you from living your best life?

_____

_____

_____

_____

In what ways could making decisions based on your own beliefs enable you to live a life that reflects your beliefs and values?

_____

_____

_____

_____

Chapter 3

HOW GROWTH WORKS

'The secret of change is to focus all of your energy, not on fighting the old, but on building the new.'
– *Dan Millman*, Way of the Peaceful Warrior: A Book That Changes Lives

What is growth? Simply put, growth is progression. Whether it's gaining confidence, saying yes to doing a presentation, learning a language, applying for a new job, asking someone out on a date or doing something new, any step towards progression is growth in action. Growth doesn't need to be represented by massive changes, but it takes you forward or reinforces a life that works for you in some way, big or small.

Growth also allows you to create, or upgrade to, a new reality. To do this consistently, you must get to know yourself, understand how you work and put a structure in place for enjoying your life on your own terms.

So, how does growth work?

The growth equation

There are two parts to the growth equation: self-awareness and self-discipline. Self-awareness is the ability to evaluate yourself objectively and self-discipline is the motivation to create structure around things that are good for you.

The confluence of the two will be the foundation for your growth.

Self-awareness: understanding how you work

How you think defines what your life looks like.

Self-awareness is simply understanding how you think, act and communicate, and the impact that has on what you have in your life. Do you ask for what you need, or do you shy away from asserting yourself? Do you blow up like an emotional bomb when you're under the pump at work, or do you calmly get on with it? Do you eat your stress, or do you run it away? Do you make plans and get overwhelmed, or do you break down goals into small steps? There is no right or wrong with any of these scenarios. They simply outline the role you (yes YOU) play in what your life looks like.

You must understand yourself before you can upgrade to a life that works better for you. Before mastering anything, you have to know how it works, right? You have to know how it operates.

Similarly, learning how you 'work' – what energises you, what motivates you, what deflates you and what causes you to stagnate or experience emotional overwhelm – will enable you to feel more in control as you make changes. That's why tools of self-awareness (for example: reflection, seeking feedback, coaching on your blind spots) are so powerful. By utilising these tools, you are putting yourself in control of how you think and respond to scenarios.

Now, if you don't yet have a self-awareness practice in place, it'll be hard to develop self-discipline. The good news is that creating a practice of self-awareness is a relatively straightforward process.

In the previous chapter, we talked about how important it is to make time to reflect. It allows you to press 'pause' and look back on your behaviour and emotions, how you communicate and who you engage with. It provides you with the space to ask yourself if that's how you want to feel each day, if it contributes to your version of success and if it essentially fits with what you want more of in your life. By reflecting in this way, you can start to create a map of yourself. You'll recognise areas that piss you off and parts of your life that energise you, and you'll identify how to do things differently to take control.

Insights from this sort of reflection might include the following:

- 'Did I want to talk to my boss like that?'
- 'Did that feel good when I didn't stand up for myself today?'
- 'Why did I say yes when I wanted to say no to taking on more work?'

The other benefit of reflecting is that it provides feedback and allows you to make small edits along the way. You can begin to coach yourself by becoming aware of how you show up and what makes you act the way you do. When you are used to giving yourself small pieces of feedback, it makes you so much more powerful. You are also able to seek feedback to drive your growth, putting yourself firmly in the driver's seat of your life. In the workplace, this is often referred to as 'being coachable', which is the degree to which the employee is capable of self-reflection.

Self-discipline: taking yourself and your goals seriously

Self-discipline is simply doing what you intend. It's the tool for achieving your goals.

How often do you set an intention or goal, only to get distracted or create an excuse not to complete the task? When you let circumstance, emotional overwhelm or blame get in the way of your goals, you enable yourself to keep doing, being or having precisely what you currently do, are or have. You become stuck.

For years, I found myself giving my power away and making excuses instead of looking after myself. The old, comfortable narratives of 'I'm too tired to exercise' or 'I'm too busy to take a break' were on loop – big time. I'd burn out, or I'd get so exhausted that I couldn't take on more responsibility or grow my business (which I was desperate to do). As a result, I'd get stuck in a loop of busy–busy, exhausted–exhausted, blah boring blah!

Guess what this enabled me to keep having? The same identity. I knew myself as someone who was always 'burned out' or 'too tired', and the idea of creating a new identity was overwhelming – so much so that I wasn't even conscious of the reality I was creating for myself until I started working with coaches who helped me reflect on it.

I was lacking a few things:

- the courage to step into a new identity without knowing what it would be
- the mental discipline to see that the structure I applied to my work could also apply to my mental and physical health
- the understanding that by starving my brain and body of exercise and rest, I was limiting my mental bandwidth,

poisoning the organ that enabled my success (my brain) and, by proxy, actively sabotaging my success. Ouch.

As a result, I found myself in identity limbo for a while. (Watch my TEDx talk, 'How to break up with your Public Identity', to see me work this out in real time!)

I needed to step outside of my comfort zone ('I'm so tired!') and see this for what it was – an excuse, not a reality – and acknowledge I was enabling myself to stay 'safe' and small.

I was convincing myself to keep being tired, keep my business small, keep my relationships non-existent and keep my capacity to earn a better living low.

As a result of a lack of self-awareness, I lacked the self-discipline to book the gym sessions, go to bed before midnight and remind myself to eat for sustained energy. It sounds so simple, but in reality, a lack of self-discipline directly affected my ability to self-actualise.

Since these uncertain times, I've taken a look around and noticed a disparity between those who do the work to achieve their goals and those who complain that they aren't where they want to be. Those who do the work opt to learn about themselves, and hold themselves accountable. They have the awareness to know what makes them motivated and deflated, and they have the discipline to talk themselves out of making excuses. They have the ability to self-coach during times when they feel stuck or overwhelmed and take small steps despite the circumstances. They don't let circumstances affect the pursuit of their goal. They commit to the process, always keeping the goal in mind, rather than giving up when the goal doesn't materialise straight away. They know growth is a day-by-day, hour-by-hour process of challenging yourself to show up.

All discipline stems from self-awareness. Master that and you'll master anything in life.

Shy away from self-awareness and, well, you'll be stuck with whatever you've got right now. Everything in your life is a direct reflection of how you think. (Gulp!)

You can choose to see this as an intimidating concept, or you can let it be the 'intel' you need to align what you want with what you have and fill in any gaps. I implore you to shift from blaming others or yourself to empowering yourself and others through your growth evolution.

Your goals are all possible. If you have a goal you haven't realised, it's likely because you don't know yourself well enough (yet), or you don't have a structure in place to support taking action steps to get you to where you want to go. We'll tackle both of these in the Growth Cycle.

Figure 1: The Growth Cycle

Own it!
- Audit your life
- Decide what to step away from
- Identify thought patterns

Take the first step
- Create a personal agreement
- Find safe ways to fail
- Reframe lingering fears
- Celebrate the small wins

Find your way back
- Create your own reflection practice
- Remember happy you
- Describe excellent you
- Design your own catchphrase!
- Identify what's changed

The Growth Cycle

Step 5 · Step 1 · Step 2 · Step 3 · Step 4

Game plan
- Do a People Audit
- Prioritise your actions
- Identify roadblocks
- Add healthy accountability

What do you want?
- Clarify what you want
- Identify blockages
- List your non-negotiables
- Create your own definition of success

The five steps of growth

In Part 2 of this book, we take a deep dive into the Growth Cycle, looking at each of the five steps in turn. Here, I want to give you an overview of the five steps in the Growth Cycle.

Step one: Own it!

When you own something, you become accountable.

The first step to growth is accepting where you are right now. There's power in stopping, or pressing 'pause', and drawing a proverbial line in the sand. Otherwise you just go around in circles. Press 'pause' and reflect on where you're at now.

Accepting where you are right now is hard for so many. You ask yourself: 'Do I really have to own this? Can't someone else do it?'

The answer is, if you want to grow, you've got to own where you are right now. You have to own it to take back control of your life and steer it in a new direction.

Your situation isn't who you are: it's simply where you are right now.

As a part of this step, you'll be asked to decide what you are interested in stepping away from. This helps create separation between where you currently are and perhaps where you'd like to be. Seeing this stage of your life as temporary is incredibly powerful.

I'll also ask you to 'rank' important elements of your life from zero to ten. Yep, you'll be asked to score your life! By assigning a number to elements of your life, you will be more readily able to see them from a different perspective.

In this step, you are going to reflect on the people and circumstances – and your responses to them – that have contributed to the way you feel or experience life right now.

The objective of this step is to identify a series of patterns that led you to where you are now and help you answer the question, 'How did I get here?'

We all want to feel in control of our life. This step is very calming and helps you take ownership, a critical part of a successful growth evolution.

Step two: Find your way back

As part of this process, I'll also ask you to reflect on the last time you felt fantastic – when you felt 'yourself', at peace with the world and fulfilled. I help you create your own reflection practice to support you with this. You'll be asked to describe this time: what the circumstances were, who surrounded you and what choices were made. As part of this, I'll also invite you to create your own catchphrase to illustrate this awesome part of your life. This process will be incredibly energising and, for many of you, you'll easily make connections between that time and why you may feel a little different now.

You are going to go through a process that acknowledges that how you got to where you are right now was no accident. It took a series of actions and reactions, good and bad. Understanding what these have been, and are, is critical for taking the power back. When you understand the role you and others play in directing your life, you are empowered to make decisions that serve you. And only you will know what that looks like for you. This is key to taking ownership. Without ownership, there can be no long-term, sustainable growth.

As part of this process, you will have an opportunity to go a little deeper in an advanced section. In this section, you'll be invited to reflect on what has changed since feeling your best.

Some of you will find this process straightforward and cathartic. Others may find it confronting and daunting, and may experience a range of emotions. This is absolutely normal. As a result, I urge you to take your time with it, and at any juncture, connect with a professional, trusted friend or coach to help you step through these steps. Just remember: this process is designed to be taken at your pace, no one else's. You are in control of this process and how far you are comfortable going. You can start, then pause, and come back at any time that works for you. Many of my clients revisit these tools at different stages of their life as their circumstances and needs change.

Step three: What do you want?

This step is a game-changer. Taking the time to clarify and articulate what you really want is so empowering. At first, it might feel daunting. However, as I mentioned earlier, there is no race to this process, and unpacking what you really want can take some work.

You can't ask for what you want if you have only a vague idea of what success looks like. In this step, you'll be defining what success looks like to you and what you want to have, feel and achieve. Some of my clients action just one area of success before making other edits to their life. Other clients do a full renovation of their lives in a short period of time. The point is, you don't need to have a perfect idea of how you will step into your growth, but you can't do anything worth doing if you aren't clear on what you want.

As a part of this step, you'll outline which of those wants are short-term goals and which are long-term goals. From there, you'll be invited to reflect on what a small stepping stone towards taking action could look like. Then you'll be able to outline what potential habit or regular action on your part could set you up for success.

It's natural at this juncture to experience feelings of uncertainty, or even the desire to back out of the process! You will certainly not be alone if you do feel this way. To counter those feelings, at this step you will also be asked whether any thoughts are cropping up that are causing you to feel uncertain. By doing this, we are identifying potential blockages sabotaging your future success. You'll be given prompters to shift fear-based statements into action-based ones.

Once you've clarified your 'I Want' List, and outlined any potential blockages, I will ask you to outline what you are willing to compromise on. This helps you create achievable goals as it manages your expectations along the way. You'll be asked to reflect on what is non-negotiable for you and what you are more flexible on.

Finally, you'll be invited to create your own definition of success. When you create your own definition of success, you also are able to create your own definition of failure. This is a hugely empowering step as it enables you to achieve success on your own terms. This very step puts you in control of your life! To support you with that, I ask you to consider ways in which you can be compassionate towards yourself as you evolve, and give yourself a pep talk when needed!

Step four: Game plan

Studies have shown that you are more likely to achieve your goals if you write them down. There are a few reasons for this. From a neurological perspective, the act of writing down how you're going to achieve something moves it from your short-term memory to your long-term memory. You are also more likely to remember something that you create than something you read.

The game plan also includes a prioritisation process, where you decide what to let go of first and who you can enlist to support you as you go through the process.

As a part of this, you'll be invited to complete a People Audit. Yep, that's right! You'll have a chance to identify what parts of your network (or future network!) will help you to succeed. This is a helpful exercise as it outlines your current cheerleaders and also makes you aware of anyone you might benefit from spending a little less time around so you can really shine!

Typically, when my clients are asked to put pen to paper and commit, guess what happens: more excuses come up! These, of course, are based on real fears. If this crops up for you in this process, I've also included a reflection exercise to help you identify whether these are real obstacles and apply problem-solving techniques.

Finally, to bring your game plan to life, you'll be invited to select what type of accountability suits your personality and what motivates you best. Some people love a deadline. Others find huge confidence teaming up with others to complete their goals. You'll be invited to select which types of accountability are the best for you, and focus on the tactical steps you need to take to bring what you want to life. By applying a safety-first approach to planning, you'll be invited to decide what small steps will give you momentum in a way that feels empowering.

By the time you get to the game plan, you'll have done the majority of the thinking work and will be ready for action.

Step five: Take the first step

The final step is to... act! In this section, you'll be asked to take action.

I invite you to create a personal agreement with yourself, linking your game plan to what's truly important to you.

Fear loves to take centre stage as we extend to our learning zone, so if you do notice any lingering fears or new 'helpful' ideas or thoughts coming up for you that are encouraging you to stay small, I outline ways to reframe those into practical steps forward in this step too.

Finally, I invite you to outline how you plan to celebrate once you have taken your first steps, or completed your first action from your 'I Want' list. Planning to win is just as powerful as planning to fail. By outlining how you will celebrate, it'll inspire you to take action for what you can gain and it'll also teach you how to plan for the best possible outcome, in life and in work.

And, as growth is cyclical, all going well you'll outgrow elements of your life again. This is a good thing. It's the gift of continually learning.

It's all a part of the process and a huge validation of the hard work you've done committing to the VIP that is you.

***

In this section, you learned the five steps to finding more in your life. I find it helpful to remind my clients during this process that no one is sitting on the sidelines, or in your Instagram, or next to your desk, or beside your journal, or in your therapy sessions, watching you do this process and expecting updates. Do these exercises and reflections at your own pace and, when you need it, seek support to guide you through these exercises from professionals and people you trust.

PART 2 GROWTH CYCLE: A STEP-BY-STEP GUIDE

GROWTH CYCLE: A STEP-BY-STEP GUIDE

Congratulations, you've arrived at the core of the book. This is where you will take practical steps towards getting more in your life!

Go through it at your own pace. There is no race here, only progress.

As a guide, my clients typically find reflecting on one 'big' question a week helps them take small, safe steps of progress.

As this book comprises five steps, you can safely dedicate a few months to making progress on your personal growth.

Some of you may find yourself soaring through the exercises, and that's great too. If that's the case, resist the temptation to focus on what you already may have clarity on. Instead, I urge you to focus on the questions that stretch you into your learning zone and towards what you want more of.

At any stage during the process, you can visit rachelservice.com, where I have supporting resources and videos for you to access and refer to.

Chapter 4

STEP ONE: OWN IT!

To eliminate things that don't make you feel great, you've first got to identify the problems. You have to edit what doesn't make you happy to make room for the good stuff. To do this, I'm going to show you how to complete an audit of your life!

Auditing your life

In this section, you are going to rate elements of your life and give each a score from zero (where you feel least comfortable or disagree most strongly) to ten (where you feel most comfortable or agree most strongly). Then I'll ask you a series of questions so that you can work out what contributed to that score. The objective is to gain greater clarity as to which elements of your life are yet to be optimised.

Once you have clarity on three areas of your life that are really working for you, and up to three areas of your life you're curious to edit, we can put a line in the sand from where you are today. It's really important to acknowledge this separation of self from circumstance as a temporary state. You are not trapped. You have complete control over what you choose to do next.

Self-reflection

Rate your level of comfort or satisfaction with each category below with a score from 0 (lowest) to 10 (highest). Leave blank any categories that don't apply to you.

Area	Category	Score
Network	Friends	
	Family	
	Partner/intimate relationship(s)	
	People I live with	
	Professional network	
	Direct manager	
	Colleagues (in my team)	
	Colleagues (out of my team)	
	People I engage with every day/week	
	Peers (e.g. cultural/spiritual/religious community)	
	Other (e.g. agent, book club, parents group)	
Work	Type of work	
	Working environment	
	Behaviour rewarded at my workplace	
	Level of trust I experience	
	Level of autonomy I experience	
	Level of accomplishment I experience	
	Type or frequency of recognition	
	Level of mastery I experience	
Mental health	I feel confident	
	I have autonomy	
	I have a healthy level of self-esteem	

Area	Category	Score
Mental health	I experience mastery (feelings of being competent at something outside of work)	
	I have boundaries in place to protect my time/energy/finances/creativity/sanity	
	I enjoy regular, quality personal/alone time	
	My self talk is positive	
	I have a positive relationship with my looks/body/physicality	
	I feel listened to	
	I can ask for help	
	I have an outlet (a person or group of people) where I can express my point of view	
	I feel comfortable sharing my point of view	
	I have an outlet for frustration or questions about life	
Physical health	I don't feel short of breath	
	I have a reason to be regularly active, either through deliberate or incidental exercise	
	I don't have ailments I have not had checked out	
	I don't feel uncharacteristically tired or unlike my 'usual' self	
	I don't experience regular symptoms of aches and pains that I have not had checked out or am not managing	
	I am up to date with my check-ups and family history of physical health and disease	
	I have everything in place to ensure that I am able to do what I want to do	

Area	Category	Score
Environment	I feel energised by my home environment	
	I feel calm and safe in my home	
	I feel 'at home' in my home	
	I am able to re-energise in my home	
	My preferences for my living space are not compromised or in conflict with others'	

With this data, we can get to work. Review your answers:

- Which categories were the top scorers (over seven out of ten)?
- Which scored six out of ten or lower?
- Which scored three out of ten or lower?
- Which categories surprised you the most?
- Which reinforced your views?

Now you are going to list three categories you are *not* going to change. These should be any you ranked from a seven to a ten.

1. _____
2. _____
3. _____

Review the categories that scored six out of ten or lower. Choose up to three you would like to work on. You are welcome to list more than three of course, but for now we are limiting our focus to three to minimise overwhelm, as you will be asked to take action on all of these categories throughout the growth process. So, start small, and you can always add more as you go and your confidence and/or capacity grows.

1. _____
2. _____
3. _____

Owning where you are right now

Many of my clients enjoy attaching a 'catchphrase' to describe where they are right now. This helps them create a proverbial line in the sand symbolising today being the last day they are going to feel like they do currently.

I'd like you to think of your catchphrase now. One benefit of doing this is that it enables you to create psychological distance from your situation, remind yourself of your role in your situation (because you aren't what happens to you, you are what you choose to do next), and focus on the positives moving forward.

Another benefit is that it enables you to be more compassionate towards your past self, as opposed to seeing your past self as 'less than' who you are today or who you will become. They are all important parts of you, and none are more or less worthy or valuable. You simply evolve and choose to respond differently as you attain more life experience and confidence.

Here are some examples from my clients, using my name instead of theirs for privacy:

'In this moment, I am choosing to step away from:

- *non-creative Rachel*
- *workaholic Rachel*
- *busy Rachel*
- *bored Rachel*
- *curious-what-else-is-out-there Rachel*
- *exhausted Rachel.*

I am going to do this by ensuring I look after my family, my personal time and my level of mastery at work. I am going to focus on working on my communication with my partner, saying no to work that isn't part of my job, and making time to exercise once a week.'

Self-reflection

If you were to assign a catchphrase to where you are right now, based on your top three and bottom three, what would it be? This catchphrase will be what you refer to when reminding yourself what you are walking away from as you walk towards a new reality.

In this moment, I am choosing to step away from:

_____

_____

_____

_____

_____

I am going to do this by prioritising [top-ranked categories 1, 2, 3]

_____

_____

_____

_____

… and editing [low-ranked categories 1, 2, 3]

_____

_____

_____

_____

Before we wrap up this section, you might like to do some further, more advanced reflection.

Optional advanced self-reflection

As you know, the only thing you can control is what you choose to do next. In the below exercise you are invited to reflect on what role you played in creating your current situation. This is designed for advanced readers who have an awareness of the fact that they play a role in the dynamics of their situation and are comfortable proceeding with this level of enquiry. (Gulp!)

While you do not always create your own circumstances, how you choose to respond to them creates your next reality. This is a helpful reflection to start developing your self-awareness and taking ownership. It helps you examine your influence on your reality.

Circle the sentence(s) below that might apply to your unique situation:

Is it possible…

> … I stayed too long in a situation?
>
> … I allowed others' expectations to dictate how I showed up?
>
> … I played a role in enabling my or others' behaviour?
>
> … I contributed to drama or fanned proverbial flames?
>
> … I chose to show up as my defensive, unhelpful or child-like self?
>
> … I leaned into fear instead of courage?
>
> … I reverted to a habit that no longer serves me?
>
> … I took on responsibility for something that is not mine to own?
>
> … I contributed to my current reality in some other way?

The goal here is not to blame ourselves, but rather to separate ourselves from our actions so that we can see that when we have awareness, we also have choices. You can thank your past self for wanting to keep you safe and protected.

Now, you might invite another reflection: what could I choose to do differently with this new-found awareness? It is not what happens to us that defines us – it's what we choose to do next that shapes our lives. When we know better, we can do better.

Making friends with your patterns

How you think influences everything – how you behave, how you communicate and, therefore, what you receive and achieve in life.

Unless you have undergone a deep self-reflection practice with a trained professional, it's pretty likely that you have never had the opportunity to become more self-aware about how you communicate and behave. More commonly – and certainly this is the case with my clients – you've had a realisation that your current reality is something you don't want to tolerate any longer. As a result, you are doing some deep introspection.

As you go through this process, look for behavioural or communication patterns that could reinforce a negative world view or a belief that something is 'not possible'. Anything is possible. It might not be easy, but anything is possible when we get out of our own way and use our patterns for good, as opposed to limiting ourselves.

In table 1, I have listed common behavioural and communication patterns I work on with my clients, and I've included my own examples.

Table 1: Common behavioural and communication patterns

Belief	As a result, I...	As a result, I don't...	I show others I believe this by...	I reinforce my belief is correct, or safe, by...
Busy = good.	work, constantly.	take holidays. say yes to social engagements. communicate boundaries at work. plan to celebrate. focus on milestones. deliver quality work.	saying how busy I am. being unavailable for important personal or social moments.	telling myself there's so much to do.
Only people who are X do what I want to do.	procrastinate.	take action towards my goals.	criticising those who do what I want to do.	placing those people on a pedestal.
I don't know enough to do X.	do as much research as I can.	take action. challenge my assumptions. reframe my fear of failure.	talking about it, but not doing anything about it.	continuing to study, or research, or read more until I am qualified 'enough'.
I'm so stressed.	keep busy.	stop to reflect on whether it is stressful or whether it's my stress response. clarify what is stressful. tune into my fight, flight or freeze response. ask for help. clarify expectations. meditate.	talking about how stressful work is. sighing in meetings or making excuses as to why I am not prepared. nurturing an environment of chaos or mess in my physical or digital space.	seeking the company of other people who complain, or see the negative in life or work. seeking those who also don't find joy in their work. pushing away people who are optimistic by making fun of them.

Behind any belief systems are experiences that have shaped you. If you are interested in reviewing why you think what you think, and unpacking what has influenced those beliefs, I strongly encourage you to seek the guidance of a trusted professional who can provide the space and expertise to help you understand this safely and in confidence. I am not looking to 'fix' you. Nope. I am simply inviting you to get curious about your DNA and how much your wiring influences how you think and behave, which therefore influences you achieving your goals.

Self-reflection

Now it's your turn. What are some of your core beliefs, or 'aha' moments, around what you've discovered about yourself during this process?

Belief _____

_____

As a result, I do… _____

_____

As a result, I don't… _____

_____

I show others I believe this by… _____

_____

I reinforce my belief is correct, or safe, by… _____

_____

Congratulations on completing step one in the growth cycle. Next, you're going to start to find your way back!

Chapter 5

STEP TWO:
FIND YOUR WAY BACK

'Ka mua, ka muri.'
'Walking backwards into the future.'

– Māori proverb

In the lead up to my TEDx talk, I was energised and focused. I had a goal, an opportunity, and I was learning every time I rehearsed. It felt great!

Following the talk, I was on a high. I loved every moment.

A few days later, however, I started to feel really flat and didn't know why. I sure didn't feel like working. I found it hard generating excitement for things that used to give me joy. I'd move like a zombie from my laptop, do the bare minimum, and go downstairs to my local cafe to read. Without the deadline, the stretch goal and urgency, I couldn't muster the energy for anything, really.

I now know I experienced what experts refer to as 'arrival fallacy'. This is the feeling you experience when you achieve a goal and there is no more goal to 'achieve'. The reason I was experiencing that flatness was because planning the talk felt so exciting. The adrenaline of actually delivering the talk was electric! Then… it was all over. After the joy of adrenaline and a big deadline, suddenly there was no big goal ahead of me to assign my energy to.

I needed to diversify my joy portfolio.

I shared this with my coach. With their guidance, I reflected on times I'd started new projects after feeling this way.

During this reflection process, I learned a lot about the role of my internal patterns. In the past, I had created a set of rules around how to keep 'busy'. Now, I was learning how to rewire a belief I had that if work wasn't stressful, I wasn't working hard enough. Through reflecting, and having a trusted ally (my coach) reflect back to me what they were hearing, I noticed that my old pattern of keeping busy, which I'd reinforced for years, was no longer serving me. Burnout – it's expensive, you know.

In this moment, I was reminded of two lessons about growth:

1. What you crave is almost always a reflection of what is lacking in your past or current life.
2. To move forward and create a future you are excited about, you must first understand your past and what makes you 'you'.

Understanding how experiences in your life have shaped who you are, your belief system and how you think, and therefore how you make decisions about your life and who you choose to populate your life with, enables you to rewire your brain to belief systems that reflect who you have become and who you want to be.

By understanding what has contributed to you becoming you, you are essentially creating a map of how your beliefs, hopes and fears were created.

Instead of absolving yourself of responsibility, through understanding your past you can instead take ownership and say, 'I am who I am because of what I have experienced and what I chose to do next.'

Remembering you

Reflection is critical to our growth. If we don't understand ourselves, we can't make decisions that serve us.

Education experts say that we don't learn solely by doing but also by reflecting. After all, we have to understand the manual before we can drive the car. We have to get the keys before we can open the door.

Developing our analytical skills and applying new information to our unique situation helps us create an awareness of how to take on new information. The act of 'looking back' literally helps our brainpower increase. Isn't that amazing? We live our lives in the present but only understand them by looking back.

The goal of reflection is to analyse not your worth but how much value your actions, beliefs and behaviours contribute to your happiness. (Oof!)

Hindsight enables you to look back to find clues to better understand yourself. Reflection creates psychological distance so that you can see yourself as independent of your situation. Studies have discovered that by creating mental distance from your reality, you can lower the perceived difficulty of a task. It helps you see your behaviour, thoughts and actions as separate from your identity and inherent worth. Without it, you 'become' your actions (creating a sense of lacking), rather than the director of those actions (creating a sense of self-empowerment).

The foundations of growth are self-awareness and self-discipline. Reflection binds these foundations through separation of self from actions.

Why we avoid reflection

The truth hurts, they say. Reflecting requires us to acknowledge our role in our reality.

Reflection is so important as it highlights what so many of us don't like to admit: our growth and mental freedom are not contingent on what someone else does or says. It is 100 per cent contingent upon our ability to self-lead.

With great opportunity comes great responsibility. And to be quite frank, not all of us can be bothered. Who wants to reflect on behaviour they're not proud of or don't fully understand? This requires a degree of ownership, and that sounds like work to many of us (and it is, no doubt about it!)

Yet reflection is the secret weapon when it comes to taking any type of positive action. It is the non-negotiable process that is required to attain personal growth in any area of your life.

As there is not (yet!) a dialogue around how reflection supports personal growth, and the power we all have to make positive steps with thoughtful enquiry, there are billions of people unaware of how their actions influence their life.

Reflection is the tool that creates psychological distance between our actions and our sense of worth. This important separation – our behaviour from our identity – enables us to see our actions as separate from ourselves, and therefore easier to edit. We aren't what we do. We are so much more than that. Our actions simply reflect choices, and those choices typically come from our comfort zones, from what we know.

I'll give you a personal example.

In anticipation of socialising recently, trying on my suits required me to face the reality of my quarantine weight gain. Too many Uber Eats orders and watching Netflix each evening adds up over six months.

I am not a bad person for gaining weight. The curry is not inherently bad. It is inherently yum. Too many curries equals tighter pants. There is no 'good' or 'bad' person here, just an action in my comfort zone that is at odds with my goal: to wear my awesome fancy suits I got for work that I love to do.

Now that life is somewhat stabilising, I have the capacity to reflect on the behaviour: one action serves my goals (to fit into my favourite suits for talks I love to give) and one doesn't (to have to buy new suits). With this information and perspective (and space!), I can now start to figure out what to do next.

I don't really want to give up something comforting to me. I can't really be bothered cooking again. But to grow, I must. I need to figure out how to get back into those suits that I paid mega bucks for. I need to take one small step – or just buy a bigger suit and move on with my life.

The point is that without reflection, there is no opportunity for growth.

With the information reflection gives us, we then have the power to make a choice aligned to what success looks like to us. And only you know what success looks like to you. That is the gift of growth! (Can I get an 'amen'?)

There are no rules here, and there is no 'right way' to reflect – the aim is simply to help you understand yourself a little better.

Our life is a pattern of events, and the only variable we can control is how we choose to respond. Reflection is one heck of a tool to help us enjoy the life we were born to live.

Self-reflection

Creating your own reflection practice

Here are the questions I ponder at the end of my day. Sometimes I write them down, but most often I simply reflect to myself as I brush my teeth or talk with my spouse at dinner time.

- What was the highlight of my day/week?

- What did I learn today?

- What can I pop in the 'I'm proud of this' bucket this week?

- If I had today again, what might I do differently, if anything, on reflection?

- What will enable me to 'close the week' mentally to enjoy my time off?

Remembering the happy you

Finding your way requires you to remember when you were happy and to ask yourself what factors influenced this. Perhaps it was your thoughts, or a mindset or confidence you had in yourself. Maybe it was a group of people you surrounded yourself with. I invite you to reflect on these elements in the following self-reflection exercise.

Self-reflection

Action #1: Remember happy you

To start this exercise, cast your mind back to the last time you felt energised or confident, safe and in control.

What were you doing?

_____

Where were you?

_____

Who were you with?

_____

What was the setting?

_____

What were you feeling at the time?

_____

What details do you recall – perhaps what you were wearing, what you could smell, see or hear?

_____

Do you remember what thoughts were going through your mind at that time?

_____

Take a moment to cast your eye back over this list. As you reflect on this list, what commonalities do you notice? What patterns are becoming clearer to you? For example, do you notice that the people surrounding you had a certain mindset or outlook? Do you find that the environment represented something important or valuable to you?

Now I'd like you to do something important: I'd like you to think about your agency (your ability to make a free choice) in the above situation.

- What boundaries were in place to ensure you could enjoy the above?

- What decisions did you make that contributed to the above scenario?

Finally I'd like you to answer the following questions:

- What was not present in the above scenario? Was it a certain group of people, a style of communication, a relationship dynamic, a scarcity mindset, a dependency, a feeling?

- If you could share what you have learned since, what lessons would you share with that version of yourself?

If you can't recall a time you felt energised, safe and in control, that is okay. That is a helpful step in itself. By identifying what you are feeling an absence of, you are already in a stronger position to seek those things as non-negotiables in your life moving forward. If you are interested in diving deeper and you would like to reflect on times when you have not felt those things, I strongly urge you to do this exercise with the support of a professional – someone who has demonstrated you can trust them.

Remembering the excellent you

The next step in finding your way back is to remember when you felt on top of the world, when you were the 'excellent' you. I'd like you to think of an adjective (descriptive word) or phrase to describe the person you were or felt like back then, when you were the excellent you – and pop your name in the descriptor.

Here are some examples of phrases that come to mind when I do this:

- Pink-suit-wearing, TEDx-talk-doing Rachel
- Creative Rachel who writes on the weekends
- Rachel who says no to things that no longer excite her!
- Rachel who puts up her hand to try new things
- Happy Rachel who is grateful for those who love her.

We are looking to create a positive neural pathway to that memory, so you can refer back to it as a litmus test to match your future choices against (it's much easier than it sounds, I promise).

Remember, you are taking control of your narrative, regardless of whether you've had experiences or circumstances that have been less than ideal. You are creating a separation between your situation and your identity.

Now you can try it in the exercise below.

Self-reflection

Action #2: Describe excellent you

When I was the excellent me...

I was/felt/had _____

_____

I was energised by _____

_____

I was experiencing _____

_____

I communicated _____

_____

I said no to _____

_____

I delegated _____

_____

You might find inspiration from some of these real-life examples my clients shared when I asked them to reflect on their 'excellent' time:

- 'I felt in control of my career, confident in myself, interested in my work.'
- 'I was energised by my surroundings at work and my network.'
- 'I was experiencing supportive friendships and was able to set boundaries.'
- 'I communicated my needs and they were heard.'
- 'I said no to things that weren't my bag, things that de-energised me, things and people I'd outgrown.'
- 'I delegated what I no longer needed to do to my team.'
- 'I was looking after myself and my partner who brings me great energy.'
- 'I went to the gym twice a week.'
- 'I had a pal who'd listen to me, challenge me, invite me out to coffee.'
- 'I was sleeping six to eight hours a night.'

All of these statements are exceptionally powerful.

So, what's changed?

If nothing has changed since the scenario you described above when you were the happy, excellent you, then bloody great!

However, if you don't feel as good as you used to, or would like to, something has changed. In this section, you'll itemise everything that has changed to create a checklist of things that have dampened your light or caused you to reflect.

Your challenge is to articulate what has shifted or changed since you felt excellent – or if 'excellent' is a stretch for now, perhaps when you felt most 'you' or more like yourself. Acknowledging what has changed that has taken you from where you were in the above positive situation to where you are now gives you clarity and sound perspective.

The objective is to prevent your reality from feeling overwhelming by breaking down contributing factors and ordering these thoughts so you can overcome them. For those of you who have experienced coaching or therapy, you might be quite familiar with this process. For those of you who are new to this process, it's incredibly empowering.

Here are real-life answers from some of my coaching clients to the question, 'What's changed?':

- 'I changed. I outgrew my job.'
- 'My partner had an affair.'
- 'I had children and my confidence dropped.'
- 'I stopped painting/singing/writing/working.'
- 'I took on a promotion and honestly? It's not for me.'
- 'We are reliant on one income.'
- 'I had a negative experience.'
- 'I started to unpack some of my childhood memories and it got really hard.'

- 'I got a new manager and they are incompetent/distant. I feel unsupported.'
- 'I got busy, I guess. I stopped doing things for me. There wasn't any time.'
- 'I moved to a new workplace.'

Self-reflection

Action #3: What has changed since your happy time?

Since I last felt confident/happy/secure/intellectually stimulated, these things happened:

_____

_____

_____

_____

_____

As you reflect on what changed, write it down or take note of when it took place. Was it recently? Was it a few years ago?

Since that time, or that change, what have some of the flow-on effects been? Perhaps you changed, or your world changed, and as a result you saw things differently, or started thinking or feeling differently (for better or worse). Maybe a major relationship in your life shifted. Potentially your tolerance for work changed. Your interests drifted. Things that used to not bother you now cause you frustration.

Here are some memories from my coaching clients when we worked through this exercise together:

- 'Since having my first child, I lost my confidence and I have found it really hard to get it back.'
- 'Since I got this promotion, I've hardly had time to be at home and I can't remember the last time I saw the kids.'
- 'Since I had that conversation with my colleague, I can't get my head around working here anymore.'
- 'Since I moved to a new city, work has taken up all my time and I never made time to make friends. I feel quite lonely at times.'
- 'Since I started my business, I can't find the will to care about my day job.'
- 'Since I got that piece of feedback, I can't stop thinking about it.'

From here, you are in a much stronger position to make appropriate decisions without changing your whole life, or the things that do work for you right now.

Self-reflection

What have you noticed since things changed?

Since _____

_____

I have found/felt/thought/noticed that _____

_____

_____

Some of the patterns I have observed include _____

_____

_____

As a result, _____

_____

_____

And now I am wondering/thinking/feeling _____

_____

_____

Chapter 6

STEP THREE: WHAT DO YOU WANT?

'You never change things by fighting the existing reality.
To change something, build a new model that makes the
existing model obsolete.'

– Buckminster Fuller, architect and inventor

To take control of the life you want, you have to be clear on
what truly ignites you. In this chapter, you'll work out how
you'd like your alternative, elevated or edited future to look.
Specifically, you'll be reflecting on how you want to feel, what
you need in order to feel like that and, in doing so, what you
will achieve.

Finding out what you want

While the task may look simple, it can take some deep
introspection, as I mentioned earlier, to shift from what you
feel you 'should' want towards what reflects your true wants
and desires. It is common for people to first write what they
feel they 'should' write, what they currently have/do, what they
think others will approve of or admire. I know it took me a

few goes to land on something that felt right for me. For now, try replacing any internal 'shoulds' with 'coulds', at least for this exercise. Try it on. See how it feels.

I want to feel/be

How do you want to feel every day? In the self-reflection box on page 90, write down how you want to feel at work, at home and in your everyday life. You might prefer to replace this with 'I want to be' instead of 'I want to feel', if that is more you.

Here are some ideas to get you started:

- I want to feel energised when I go to work.
- I want to feel confident at the gym.
- I want to feel competent with my finances.
- I want to feel in control of my emotions.
- I want to feel enriched by my friendships.
- I want to be supported by my peers.
- I want to be intellectually stimulated.
- I want to be surrounded by people who inspire me.

I want to have

As you reflect on what you want to have, take note of what will enable you to experience security, safety and support. When we feel safe, secure and supported, we are mentally freed up to take steps towards our self-fulfilment. (You can learn more about what we crave for our self-fulfilment in Chapter 12, where Maslow's Hierarchy of Needs is discussed.) Those of you reading this who gain fulfilment through providing for others might find this section confronting; for the purpose of this exercise, encourage yourself to focus on meeting your own needs before reflecting on how to contribute and add value to others' lives. Remember, if all your needs were currently being met, you wouldn't be reading this book!

Here are some examples of what you might want to have:

- I want to have a job I enjoy.
- I want to own my own property.
- I want to have friends who support and inspire me.
- I want to have access to mentors.
- I want to have savings.
- I want to have the confidence to say no.

I want to achieve

This can be as simple as a goal you'd like to achieve, such as securing a pay rise or being in an enriching relationship, or as large as writing a book or receiving a lifetime achievement award. The point of this section is to move your thinking towards tangible achievements that have meaning to you.

If you're feeling stuck, start with what you wanted to be or do when you were younger, then move on to what you find yourself craving now.

Here are some ideas to get you started:

- When I was a kid, I wanted to be... (an astronaut, a vet, no idea but it involved food...)
- When I was at school, I wanted to be... (a doctor, a singer, a firefighter, a yoga teacher)
- What I'd actually love to be (and I have no idea how this would become a reality) is... (Beyoncé, a performer, a scientist).

Self-reflection

	I want to feel/be…	I want to have…	I want to achieve…
Timeline: Is this a short-term or long-term goal?			
Stepping stone: What is the smallest, safest step you can take towards this?			
Habit: What long-term habit (something you do every day, or every week) could enable you to achieve this?			

I've provided some space here for you to think about how you would like to feel, what you want to have and what you want to achieve. Take your time, be compassionate with yourself as you record your thoughts, and make space for what you really want.

I think it's useful to give you some examples:

'I want to be a personal trainer.'

- *Timeline:* Long-term.
- *Stepping stone:* I need cash to fund further study. I also have lots going on with work, so the stepping stone is to put it on the list for next year. (Tell someone else about it so they keep me accountable.)
- *Habit:* Schedule to come back to this next year.

'I want my own apartment.'

- *Timeline:* Mid-term (one year).
- *Stepping stone:* Start looking around at prices. What do apartments go for these days in the location I'm keen to live in?
- *Habit:* This is going to cost me far more than my current rent. Start getting into the habit of putting away a small amount of my income towards a mortgage.

'I want to be a motivational speaker.'

- *Timeline:* The next six months.
- *Stepping stone:* Start a blog. Ask my friend what blogging platform she uses.
- *Habit:* Make room on Sundays to start writing 'how to's while I figure out what I'm doing.

- 'I want to be exercising regularly.'
- *Timeline:* It's pretty darn important, so ASAP.
- *Stepping stone:* Lower expectations. Do two workouts a week.
- *Habit:* Commit to two workouts a week for the next six weeks. See what happens.

'I want to have friends who "get" me.'
- *Timeline:* ASAP.
- *Stepping stone:* Do a People Audit (see Chapter 7).
- *Habit:* Say NO if it doesn't feel right or assess the situation before saying YES.

As you can see, stepping through the timeline, stepping stones and habits transform what you are craving into tangible steps. In the following section, you'll have the opportunity to ask yourself what you'd like to prioritise, what is realistic in your environment with your current situation and what you are ready to compromise on to experience a different reality for yourself.

But, I'm not sure about this...

It is natural to have thoughts of doubt or pushback as you undertake this exercise. In fact, I'd be surprised if you didn't! In every session I have had the privilege of leading with clients, at least one fear-based barrier comes up. If we use the acronym of FEAR (false evidence appearing real), we know this is our learning zone letting us know we are going into new territory. And that territory can feel scary at first, which is why you create blocking thoughts – excuses, really, to not pursue your hopes and dreams.

These excuses feel real, they really do. Sometimes it feels impossible to separate these fears from facts, especially if you are very new to what I am proposing or it requires a big change.

But when you take a moment to really interrogate them, something powerful starts happening. You start to see which thoughts are real and which are excuses to keep you in your comfort zone. I find this practice helpful at every stage of my growth, and it's a tool I use frequently. Every time I grow, I have moments of doubt. To this day, I go through the process of, 'Is this helpful? Is this fear speaking? Is there another way?'

Self-doubt keeps you in your comfort zone and away from success.

As you move into your game plan in the following step, addressing these will help you identify what to prioritise, what thoughts are helpful guides and what thoughts no longer serve you.

Common thought-blocking can start with:

- But...
- I don't know how to...
- I'm worried about...
- What if...

Here are examples from many of my clients and a few of my personal examples.

- But... 'I've never done this before!'; 'Where will the money come from?'; 'It doesn't exist!'; 'Who am I to do that?'; 'Aren't other people already doing stuff like this?'
- I don't know how to... 'start a business, let alone run one!'; 'have this conversation with my boss'; 'even start.'

- I'm worried about… 'what my family will think'; 'how I would make ends meet'; 'what if I'm actually successful?'
- What if… 'I can't get a new job?'; 'my boss responds negatively?'; 'they hate it?'

Self-reflection

What thoughts or blockages are preventing you from achieving success?

_____

_____

_____

_____

_____

_____

_____

_____

_____

_____

_____

_____

_____

There is merit in all of the above fears. No fear is 'wrong', but rather is a signal of what is causing us to stop before taking action. When we table what precisely is stopping us from taking action, we can reflect upon and eventually interrogate the fear. Shifting from a place of negativity to a 'how might I' statement can be particularly powerful, shifting fear-based thoughts into a 'to think about more' list.

Table 2 shows another way of moving forward with those fears as prompters, using examples from many of my clients and a few of my own.

Table 2: Turning fears into prompters

Instead of...	Try an action-based statement...
I've never done this before!	I haven't done this yet. What do I need to know before I get started? What free resources are online as a starting point?
Where will the money come from?	I'll need to think about my income. First I'll write down how much it costs to be me per month. Then I can chat to my partner, or a financial advisor, to get some further detail on commitments.
It doesn't exist!	I haven't seen any examples of what I'm thinking of doing. I wonder where else I could look for inspiration or examples? Perhaps it doesn't yet exist because someone needs to create it?
Who am I to do that?	What I know best is my personal experience and point of view. That's a helpful start for what I'm thinking of doing next.
Aren't other people already doing stuff like this?	It sure is a popular arena with lots of inspiring people doing what I'd love to do. I wonder what I could bring that's different or a fresh perspective.

Why not try with your own versions of the above? Feel free to rip out this page as a handy reminder, or write it down on a notepad or Post-it, and leave it nearby to help you as you reflect on what 'more' looks like to you.

Self-reflection

Use the table below to turn your fears into prompters.

Instead of...	My action-based statement is...
I've never done this before!	
Where will the money come from?	
It doesn't exist!	
Who am I to do that?	
Aren't other people already doing stuff like this?	

Identifying non-negotiables

We all have deal-breakers. We set boundaries, or expectations, that protect our wellbeing and happiness. To create a life of growth, you need to clarify your deal-breakers. This will help you make decisions that enable your success.

Self-reflection

Outline what you are and are not willing to compromise on in your life moving forward.

I am not willing to compromise on _____

_____

_____

_____

Thought-starters: family; relationships; health; money; flexibility; working at a certain time; movie night with my pals.

I am flexible on things like _____

_____

_____

_____

Thought-starters: where I work from; who is involved; how I start; how I get there.

I am indifferent about things like _____

_____

_____

_____

Thought-starters: working hours; location; salary.

The above exercise will help you with negotiations, including discussions with yourself and anyone who might be impacted by any significant life changes. You might enjoy doing this exercise with your significant other if you're in a committed relationship as you both evaluate how your mutual 'I Want' Lists impact each other and where you can both find room for each other's goals.

Creating your own definition of success

Now you are clear on what you want to feel/be, have and achieve, you are in a strong position to define what success looks like to you. Based on your idea of success, you are also in control of what you deem failure to look like. I urge you to make your definition of success unique to you, be compassionate and think BIG. Success is not defined by what you do, but rather what you deem to be important.

Self-reflection

Success to me is _____

_____

_____

_____

I will succeed because I have chosen to do/think/feel _____

_____

_____

_____

When I succeed, I will celebrate by _____

_____

_____

_____

_____

Failure to me is _____

_____

_____

_____

_____

If I fail, it will be because I choose/prioritise _____

_____

_____

_____

_____

If I fail, I will be compassionate by reminding myself that

_____

_____

_____

_____

To get back on track I can choose to _____

_____

_____

_____

_____

You're making great progress – well done. In the following step, you'll outline what action or prioritisation will enable your version of success and help you make decisions to minimise experiences of failure.

Chapter 7

STEP FOUR: GAME PLAN

'The people who surround us model what's possible.'

– Luvvie Ajayi

In this chapter we investigate what needs to happen for your 'I Want' Lists to become a reality.

At this juncture, you might be reluctant to act on your plans and ideas. It might start to feel hard, and you might want to quit. Fear and overwhelm can show up in all sorts of surprising ways when searching for more in your life!

If you do find yourself opting out of this step, that is okay. You might need some time to digest your needs and wants before taking action. This is your old identity trying to keep you safe. Failure is not failing to finish this exercise, it's failing to listen to what you need.

You are in control of this process. I implore you to populate your game plan at your own pace as ultimately this is about you taking control of your life. But when you are ready, do return, as this is where your life will start to shift in reflection of your introspection.

Doing a people audit

Cultivating a network of supportive people is critical to your success.

The people we spend time with have a profound impact on our energy levels, our focus, whether we activate our goals and how much we experience fulfilment on a daily basis. Colleagues, friends, housemates, gym buddies, the local barista – how people interact with you, and how you interact with them, directly affects how you feel.

In the following exercise, I invite you to reflect on who in your network enables different things in your life. It's okay if you leave some columns blank or you don't write much; the objective here is not to have a long list but rather a starting place to make decisions, set boundaries and invite new people into your life who can help you enjoy everything you have worked so hard for. Some of your network will appear in more than one category, which is great, too.

Self-reflection

Who in my network…

… supports me? *(Who supports you and is open to you developing the future you?)*

_____

_____

_____

_____

_____

_____

... teaches me? *(Who do you learn new things from? Who gives you access to a different, interesting perspective that you value?)*

_____

_____

_____

_____

_____

_____

... inspires me? *(Who demonstrates an example of your values or how you would like to live your life? This could be someone in your network or someone you follow online.)*

_____

_____

_____

_____

_____

_____

... is fun to be around? *(Who brings you joy through their presence? Who helps you laugh and see life a little less seriously?)*

_____

_____

_____

_____

_____

_____

THERE HAS TO BE MORE

The following reflection questions might help you in your thinking.

> ## Self-reflection
>
> How often do you get to see the people you have named in each of the categories?
>
> _____
>
> _____
>
> What opportunities exist to see them more frequently? Could you find ways to see them more often?
>
> _____
>
> _____
>
> Who didn't make this list?
>
> _____
>
> _____
>
> _____
>
> How often are you spending time with people who don't support, teach, inspire or bring you fun?
>
> _____
>
> _____
>
> What small tweak to your calendar or decision-making will give you more time to spend with those who support, teach, inspire and provide fun, and less with those who don't?
>
> _____
>
> _____

You don't necessarily need to cull friendships or break off major relationships with people who don't appear in these categories. Sometimes spending less time or communicating a boundary with them, or being mindful of exposure, can make all the difference to your energy levels. Exposure and frequency are your levers here, and you're in the driver's seat.

Each person is different. You might have a full exercise chart of people on your list; or, like many of my clients, you might find some columns completely empty. Don't feel disheartened. One of my clients discovered that she had a particularly empty list, and it really took her by surprise. She had lots of people in her life, but she didn't have many who reflected what she wanted more of in her life. This made her feel a bit sad at first. We worked together to see it differently. Rather than an empty list, we pondered if it was possible to see it as a VIP list, and she had space to invite a few more VIPs to her list when she met them. We also talked about the power of shifting dynamics in existing friendships. Our friends grow too, you know.

If your list looks emptier than anticipated, simply consider that you have space to look for special people to add to your VIP list. I know that as my life evolves, people can move between all sorts of lists, make appearances and evolve and grow. Simply use this exercise as a clarification of what you require to succeed, and do a mental map of how you might invite more of these sorts of people into your life or extend your networks to seek them.

You might ask yourself, could you meet new people through your work or a place of worship, or by taking up a side project or hobbies? You could reach out to someone online who you admire and ask them what groups they found useful to meet like-minded people. The main thing to remember is that, if your lists are low and empty, you are not alone. You are simply clarifying what your needs are so you can find those types of people out there.

Bringing your 'I Want' List to life

It can be helpful to break down what can seem impossible tasks into practical steps. From there, you can prioritise the tasks into important/urgent/shelve for later.

Take a look at table 3, opposite, then try this exercise to prioritise some easy wins for yourself.

Self-reflection

Easy wins: _____

_____

_____

_____

Important: _____

_____

_____

_____

Urgent: _____

_____

_____

_____

Shelve for later: _____

_____

_____

_____

Table 3: Categorising goals

Easy wins	Important	Urgent	Shelve for later
Which goals in my 'I Want' List feel easy and therefore will contribute to a sense of momentum?	Which of my 'I Want' List goals are the most important to my wellbeing?	What needs to happen to lighten the load or get me out of a pressured scenario?	Of interest, important, but not a priority right now. Pick up once I have ticked off the Urgent and Important lists. This might be the same as in the Important list.
Common examples: • Update my LinkedIn. • Apply for a part-time job. • Get out of that commitment I don't want/need to do. • Book one hour a week to work on my 'I Want' List.	Common examples: • Find a job that excites me. • Put boundaries in place with family/people who I interact with regularly.	Common examples: • Save three months' salary so I can resign. • Give my resignation letter. • Move out of my accommodation. • Communicate a boundary. • Delegate tasks.	Common examples: • Write a book. Once I have established my new job and have settled in I'd be keen to explore this. • Start a business/blog. • Have a conversation with X.

What will stop you from succeeding?

It sounds counterintuitive, doesn't it, to ask what could get in your way after inviting you to outline your 'I Want' List. In my experience working with thousands of people, I have discovered that outlining what could go wrong upfront is a powerful way to manage expectations early and set people up for success.

Imagined and real barriers to your success are the same – if you see them as barriers. It's worth being explicit with yourself about how you see your next steps. Some people refer to this as 'self-coaching'.

Typically, the limiters to success include:

- **My relationship with certainty:** I don't really want this to happen.
- **Self-efficacy/self-belief:** I don't truly believe it can happen.
- **Environment:** My environment does not endorse it.
- **Skills:** I will require new skills and knowledge.
- **Capacity:** I lack the emotional, financial or physical capacity/tools.
- **Support:** I require additional support.

The objective of the game plan step in your growth is to help you get on the front foot to manage your expectations of what could get in your way, and to make a plan to overcome those challenges.

The exercise on the next page will help.

Self-reflection

Outline what you perceive to be obstacles, if any, to achieving your 'I Want' List. You may have populated these in the section prior. Referring to that list is great, too.

_____

_____

_____

Which of the above are within your control?

_____

_____

_____

Which are out of your control and therefore require you to release attachment to them?

_____

_____

_____

Of the obstacles that are within your control or are able to be influenced by you, which are you open to approaching or learning more about how to overcome or take action on?

_____

_____

_____

Which of the above are you willing to compromise on or approach differently?

_____

_____

_____

Which of the above are you not willing to compromise on?
(These are your deal-breakers.)

_____

_____

_____

_____

What does your 'I Want' List look like now? Do you need to make any edits based on your deal-breakers and choices?

Prioritising

Now it's time to put your 'I Want' List into order of priority using the table opposite.

If the time slots don't suit you, you might prefer to list your priorities against personal milestones. These might include before or after retirement, before your 60th birthday, after your first child or after securing a salary of X dollars.

For example, my goal was to write my first book – this book – before my 40th birthday so I could create the space to share these learnings with the world in my forties. Once I turned 38, I was spurred into action.

When you get used to making a commitment to yourself, and build the trust with yourself that you can do it, it has a huge flow-on effect. Making my book-writing commitment known to others was one heck of a motivator for me. Make this list your proverbial carrot!

To endorse your list, what is the smallest action you can take to progress each goal right now?

Self-reflection

Which goal would you like to achieve/experience first, and by when?

When?	Easy win (What is the smallest step?)	Important (What is a non-negotiable?)	Urgent (What needs to be prioritised?)
Today			
This week			
This month			
This quarter			
This year			
Your own milestone:			

Adding accountability

Of course, adding accountability to your goals will help. What forms of accountability help you take positive action towards your goals? Many people find a deadline coupled with someone they respect knowing about it (an accountability buddy) to be a compelling combination.

Here are some examples to get you thinking:

- **Deadline:** The power of a deadline is hard to underestimate. My editor gave me a deadline to finish a first draft of this book by a certain date. The only person I told about it was my spouse, to explain why I needed to scurry away most evenings. After making the commitment to myself, the prospect of disappointing myself (as a perfectionist) was a huge motivator.

- **Public admission:** Aligning your reputation to your commitment is an influential motivational tool, according to behavioural experts. Declaring a deadline through public admission (for example, on social media), or telling someone you admire, can force you to reflect on what others might think if you don't take action. Telling someone your goal can help you feel a sense of responsibility to them, thereby motivating you to act. Before completing the first draft of this book, I created a website to let people know the book was coming. My ego wouldn't let me fail to hand in the draft after that public announcement!

- **Social support:** This works well for people who enjoy group activities. Teaming up with someone else who is going through a similar journey is particularly motivating due to a phenomenon known as social accountability. One study discovered that people who participated in a

weight-loss program with friends were 42 per cent more
likely to maintain weight loss due to social accountability
and 95 per cent more likely to complete the program.

- **Positive reinforcement:** Telling someone who can support
you and validate you as you pursue your goal can help you
feel supported, and therefore more likely to crave that
positive reinforcement as your confidence increases. While
supportive friends are a great start, beware of leaning on
your friends for validation. If you crave consistent positive
validation, explore the possibility of finding a coach who
can help you overcome hurdles and meet your need for
positive reinforcement.

- **Investing time:** You may find it useful to go away for a
while, to take time off work, to bunker down and make a
dent in achieving your long-term goals. This is particularly
useful if you are completing your PhD thesis, creating
a cookbook or making the time to get life admin and
finances under control. The investment of time and, in
some instances, a change of scenery achieved by going
to another location forces you to not waste it and stay
focused.

- **Cultivating a network of 'doers':** Cultivating a network
of people who embody the type of behaviour you want
to emulate will help you achieve your goals. They will be
people who take action to achieve their own goals. You
will notice those who take action towards their goals
spend less time waxing lyrical about problems they have
control over influencing and more time living a life of
peace and fulfilment.

Chapter 8

STEP FIVE: TAKE THE FIRST STEP

'They always say time changes things, but you actually have to change them yourself.'

– Andy Warhol

You've thought about it. You've done the exercises. You have your game plan. You've told people you love. What else do you need?

You need the confidence to take the first step.

If this feels scary, that's okay. It's sensible to pause before taking action, generally speaking. But at some point, you do need to meet the commitment you made to yourself and be brave enough to take one step forward.

Your personal agreement

Sometimes we stall on doing things that are good for us because we're overwhelmed. If you feel this way, you can reframe a scary step into one that is good for you by reminding yourself of your agreement with yourself and the expectation you are moving towards. The process of outlining what commitments you are making to yourself, and getting into the habit of celebrating your wins, will be a lifelong skill.

As you make changes to your life, it is important to remind yourself that the only person you need to please is yourself. This is easier if you know what deal you are making with yourself. For that reason, I invite you to make a deal with yourself as a sort of guiding principle to help you keep momentum.

The saying goes that vague questions get vague answers. By challenging yourself to be specific, you are setting yourself up for success. So, reflect on what commitments you have made to the most important person in your life – you.

Here are some questions I invite you to ask yourself at this stage.

Self-reflection

What am I no longer willing to tolerate?

_____

_____

What standard or precedent am I setting for myself?

_____

_____

What old thoughts no longer take me to where I am going?

_____

_____

What will I replace these with to succeed?

_____

_____

These are big questions, but they can be answered succinctly. Examples I have received from my clients over the years, and from my own work, include:

- As a people leader, I am no longer willing to tolerate incompetence in my team. Competence is my responsibility to find, to manage and to manage out if required.
- The precedent I am setting for myself is to become the first entrepreneur in my family. It will mean challenges ahead, but I am setting an example to my children that anything is possible.
- By thinking small, I am robbing myself of what I know I want. Thoughts about not being good enough do not fit where I am going.

Think about your own answers. This is a very powerful exercise, and I invite you to reflect on your answers regularly and adapt them as you grow. In a sense, you are creating boundaries for yourself to keep yourself accountable.

If you have the privilege of managing or raising others, I invite you to pose these questions to support their growth. Everyone wins when they have agency and permission to grow.

What to expect as you make changes

Something they don't tell you when you make changes is that sometimes it takes a while for your brain to catch up to your new reality. It's a phenomenon called cognitive dissonance. This is when you experience your own contradiction, or the inconsistency of two contradictory beliefs within your own mind. This can happen when you evolve your thinking, and intellectually you agree with a concept but your belief system needs a little while to catch up with the fact that it is real. You need cold, hard evidence.

Many of my clients describe a feeling where they make a change, they get what they want, and all of a sudden they think, 'Oh no! Something is going to go badly soon.' This is because, while intellectually they agree with the choice they've made, their belief system doesn't *yet* match their new reality. Their subconscious is searching for proof that it was a good idea so it can create their new comfort zone.

I'll give you a personal example. Recently I hired a great team member. They were so talented that, after a few months, I offered them even greater responsibility – so much so that I was able to free up valuable time to work on the business, not in the business.

Despite intellectually understanding this, financially supporting this through paying their salary each month, and emotionally understanding this by trusting their talent implicitly, for some reason I couldn't stop doing administration. I'd jump in to 'save the day', or 'rescue' a project that needed (or so I thought!) my expertise.

My team member, to their credit, would gently, warmly and thoughtfully ask whether it was something they could do, and whether that would give me my time back to focus on the big-picture tasks.

'Oh my goodness,' I remember thinking. 'I'm doing everything to keep myself and my business small. I want to operate at a higher level, but part of me thinks I don't deserve to not be busy all the time'.

Aha! The gift of reflection strikes again.

It took me weeks to start to believe what I was saying, and indeed investing in, on a deeper level. I wanted the support, I just didn't know how to be the new version of me with that support. I didn't know what to do when I wasn't being so thinly stretched. I wanted to evolve my identity, but my subconscious was simply trying to keep me safe with what I knew best: keeping busy! Delegation truly is an art form.

Through reflecting on why I was saying one thing and doing another, I was able to reconcile my cognitive dissonance. I was able, as a result, to actively focus on retraining my brain to think about the following new statements:

- When I invest time into working on the business, I grow the business. When I invest time into working in the business, I keep the business, and myself, small. I disempower the amazing people I have hired to grow the business.
- By growing the business, I am providing for my team and my clients. I am growing people's businesses, careers, lives and bank accounts when I show up and focus on the big picture.
- I am not letting my team down when I focus on the business. Rather, I am paving the way.

Do you see the difference?

Manifestation experts say that in this moment – the moment between an old belief and a new one – it is critical to temporarily suspend belief and judgement to enable yourself to step into your new reality.

You might think this sounds a little odd, but go with me here.

Your reality is so often a reflection of your fears, not your true desires. Read that again! Your reality expands to the level of your fears, not your desires. You are always trying to find ways to keep yourself safe.

So, when you create the space for a new reality to occur, in steps your brain seeking certainty. You will want certainty as you grow, and at some stages it is not always possible.

To really grow, you need to have a little faith that might sometimes defy logic. It might not seem 'possible' at first. 'This can't be real,' your fearful self might whisper. 'You know this is not possible,' your former self might say.

As your mindset catches up with your new reality, know that there are a number of tools you can put in your toolkit to ensure you feel safe and supported along the way. And one of these is having a little faith that while you might not understand it yet, by creating the space to allow a change in your life, and by taking small steps of action, committing to change and investing in the future, you are creating an entirely new reality.

For example, while growing my business, I knew it would be a tremendous help to have support, but I just couldn't see how I could make it happen. It felt like there was no time. That and, in the early days, I simply couldn't afford help! I was too busy figuring out how to pay myself.

When COVID-19 hit, demand for Happiness Concierge exploded. I needed help, and fast. I hired an amazing team member, as I've described. As I documented their onboarding manual, I heard my old self say, 'I don't know what they're going to do around here', 'there mightn't be enough for them to do', and 'I hope I'm a good boss. Will I be a good boss?' Naughty old self! I offered them a part-time role, and we both decided we'd review and see how it went.

Shortly thereafter, they were adding so much value that I offered them a promotion. As the business grew, the value of their support – both to the strength and quality of our products but also to my mental health – was incalculable. I felt, quite simply, like a different person with the right support.

As mentioned earlier, it can take time to outgrow your old reality, even when intellectually you understand it's good for you. Know that even the person writing this book has trouble suspending their reality to upgrade their belief system! But gosh, does it work.

Becoming your own cheerleader

Earlier in the book I invited you to outline what success looks like to you. Remember, you are in the driver's seat of how you see success, and it can be particularly valuable to remind yourself of this during moments of doubt and overwhelm.

It can be helpful to have a few prepared reframing statements up your sleeve. These statements serve the purpose of being your personal coach, your internal cheerleader, to remind you of your definition of success.

The process I underwent earlier, to create the space for me and my team to shine, is a technique called positive reframing. The benefits of positive reframing include increased confidence, competence and ability to focus.

Take a moment to remember:

- What did you outline as your definition of success?
- What will remind you of this as you navigate this change?
- Based on this reflection, what could your 'mantra' become during moments of doubt or fear?

Table 4 shows some examples used by my coaching clients to set themselves up for success.

Table 4: Reframing thoughts

Thought	Reframed thought
'I'm not smart enough for this!'	'Being the smartest person in the room means I have nothing to learn and keeps my ego in charge.'
'I'm not an expert.'	'I don't need to be an expert. I do need to pay attention to who I'm serving or being present for and be committed to learning.'
'There are so many other people who are more qualified for this.'	'While it's true other people have more qualifications, what I am bringing to the table is my individual perspective and summary of experiences unique to me. I am not here to compete; I am here to complement others' talents.'
'I have no idea what I'm doing.'	'I am taking a step forward every day.'
'This is way harder than I thought.'	'I'd rather be learning every day than be bored.'
'I've got so much to do.'	'I don't need to do it all at once. One step at a time.'
'I don't have a plan.'	'All I need to do is make sure the steps I take make sense to me.'

Writing down your mantra, or what you'll remind yourself of during times of doubt, can help you channel your inner cheerleader and stay the course. I personally like to write mine on Post-its and put them on my computer to remind myself when I am trying something new to keep going during trying moments. Over time, these catchphrases sink in.

Finding safe ways to fail

In Chapter 1, we discussed the concept of the learning zone. This is the area where you are trying something new, stretching yourself and learning. This is exactly where you want to be.

The downside to this zone is that, in the short term, you might feel incompetent, awkward and frustrated, and at times you might even have feelings of regret. A natural part of growth is to feel uncomfortable or out of place as you get used to your new reality.

To counterbalance these feelings and experiences, it can be helpful to identify 'safe ways to fail'. I know it sounds counterintuitive, but hear me out.

Take yourself back to when you did something for the first time, or for the first time in a long time. Perhaps it was your first job as a teenager. Maybe you were returning to the workforce after an extended break. It might have been the time you experienced the awesome responsibility of loving someone.

Chances are, when you were doing something like this for the first time, it took you a decent chunk of time to get your head around what your responsibilities were. You probably didn't feel in control. In fact, in the workplace, it can take three to six months on average for a new starter to get up to speed in a new role – let alone in a new career, or when making a change in their life!

Failing privately simply means trying out something new in a safe space. By failing with a buffer, you give yourself an opportunity to stretch yourself without implicating anyone else. You get to try on ideas and moves for size behind the scenes. It's the first step to mastery: taking yourself seriously enough to practise.

I'll share an example of failing safely in the workplace. At Happiness Concierge, we often create a dress rehearsal with people in the business or our extended network. We let them know we are testing out new content and are looking for feedback on what they find helpful or effective. This session, held privately and in advance of releasing the initiative publicly, helps us understand where we are on track and where changes need to be made. Doing this discovery privately, away from paying clients, means that when we do present new content or launch new products, they get to experience the polished, finished, best possible product.

Let's take another example. If I have to have a constructive conversation at work, I regularly rehearse my talking points with my coach. By having a private conversation about someone I care about, I am getting feedback on how to make sure I am clear, kind and specific.

When applying this context to life, and to changes that impact our lives, it will take some time to get used to a new routine. That means the first few times you try something new, it might not land as you might wish. It might be awkward, and you might wonder – as American radio host Ira Glass has so aptly spoken about in the past – how to answer the challenge of, 'I want to be better than this but I don't know how to be better than this.' The answer is simply execution. By creating ways to execute – or do what you want to do more of – more regularly over time, your skill increases. I suggest that by creating ways to express yourself privately before you go 'live' or 'public', you can create a bank of experience that helps you become more confident as time goes on.

Creating a group of people you can 'fail safely' with is a wonderful way to do this. It opens a dialogue around new ideas and gives you permission to not need to be perfect – or actually any good – at first. This group might comprise your coworkers in your immediate team, your most compassionate friends, a new group of people you meet online or someone you simply feel comfortable with.

The only way you get better at something is to do it, and keep doing it until it becomes second nature. Be kind to yourself as you find your feet. It'll take some time, and it's time worth investing in to help you land on your feet confidently.

You may feel resentment

Returning to the previous question, 'What can you expect as you make changes?', I'd like now to discuss resentment. As you move towards the new you, it's very natural to start to feel resentment towards people you love, or loved.

You may have already begun the process of creating space between yourself and people who no longer provide support to you in a way that serves you.

After the adrenaline of putting a boundary into place, you may experience a pretty hefty dose of resentment. You'll feel like this typically after you've taken some space from the situation or person, and this time away gives you clarity. With this clarity can come some pretty epic truth bombs. For this reason, you may start to hurt in a different way. And one common way that hurt can show up is through anger, frustration or resentment towards someone you used to have a close relationship with (healthily or not!).

From working 60-hour weeks to saying no with confidence

I have a client who was working 60-hour weeks. She had a team to delegate to, but she found herself doing the work her team was supposed to be doing, and she was exhausted. She felt perpetually behind and like she never had any time for herself.

As she started to learn about her role in the situation (saying yes to everything was her default as a chronic people-pleaser), she started to feel the heavens open. Or was it hell? She began to feel a deep well of rage as she described the feeling of realising others were taking advantage of her kindness at work.

To paraphrase Sigmund Freud, 'Unexpressed emotions never go away. They simply get buried alive.' And now her repressed emotions were coming out thick and fast.

Her rage needed a home – a productive way to be expressed. To create space for this, she dedicated time to professional coaching, where she could work through her frustration privately, without her colleagues having exposure to it, and create a game plan.

Over time, and with practice, she shifted from frustration to making steps to feel confident in communicating her needs. She started putting boundaries in place at work. She upskilled, and learned how to effectively delegate. She learned how to 'give back' tasks before they were finished. She started saying 'no, however…' instead of 'of course!' She put hours back into her diary every week. She used techniques to buy herself time to check if a task was something that she could do before committing. Over time, the frustration dissipated and her confidence started to grow. Boundaries and confident communication became the tools to help her take ownership of her career and life.

Can you relate? Have you ever had an experience where you decided to raise your standards and realised how others have responded to your outdated ways of being or working?

The rage can be very real. Something I have personally found very helpful is to remind myself: 'No one is secretly reading your mind. You have to tell them.' Grr!

Experts tell you to 'feel your feelings'. You don't want to bottle ill feelings up, as we've discussed. You do want to take those feelings to a safe space where you won't hurt anyone else around you as you express and work through them. That is something you can control.

For those of you who are putting boundaries in place at work, this is particularly important. You don't want resentment to build up and cause you to do something or react in some way that will damage your reputation. By taking responsibility for yourself and doing the work privately to understand these feelings, you are protecting yourself from showing up in a way that is not your best self at work.

Remember, feelings are temporary. The only way to control how we feel is to work through why we feel that way, find strategies to support those feelings and then give up control by freeing ourselves from rules on how to feel. This is no small task. It takes time to process, understand and, in some cases, heal.

To summarise, the work you do privately will show up in public ways. If you choose to not lean into that deeper enquiry, you run the risk of it showing up in ways you may later regret. Alternatively, if you find a safe place to step through your experience, you can take the power back and make decisions from a place of certainty, from a place that feels like your most secure self.

Take it from me, as someone who has learned the hard way! It's work worth doing. You don't need to rush it, but to achieve growth, you must prioritise it.

The final push

The word motivation comes from the Latin word *movere*, meaning 'to move'. When action is taken, you will feel motivated once you have taken one small step forward.

Remind yourself of what's in it for you. You don't need to be an expert in what you're about to do to take that first step. You only need to start. Help yourself by writing out what success looks like to you, what failure is according to your definition and the expectation you are setting for yourself.

Write it on a Post-it and put it on your computer, or stick a note under a fridge magnet. Take a photo of it and save it as your phone background. Write it in lipstick on your mirror. Create an alarm on your phone to have it pop up. Rip out this page of the book and sticky-tape it to your bookcase. Frame it and put it on top of your microwave. Whatever you do, make it top of mind for you to remind yourself: you have freaking got this. And you can rely on YOU.

***

We've now completed the Growth Cycle! Congratulations.

Is there more? Because of your work, yes, there is.

As you grow, not everyone will be supportive of your journey. That's why you'll need the next part of this book to support you as you navigate your next steps: your survival guide!

PART 3
YOUR
SURVIVAL
GUIDE

YOUR SURVIVAL GUIDE

On completing the Growth Cycle, you might think, 'Great, I'm done. I've done the work; now all I have to do is get on with it and tell the world.'

Know this: every change you make will have a flow-on effect on the world around you.

Some people in your life will support this. Some will feel less comfortable with the changes you are making, or are about to make.

The truth is, when you make any significant change to how you choose to live your life, you run the risk of losing a few people you might care about along the way. This can feel liberating, frustrating and heartbreaking, all at the same time.

Things are going to get tough for a bit before they get better, so I've included a thorough survival guide to help you through.

There's a range of flow-on effects that can happen, so mentally preparing yourself for how others might respond to your exciting news is a helpful step.

Chapter 9

HOW OTHERS WILL REACT TO YOUR CHANGE

Some people you love might freak out

I remember so vividly doing the work to make changes that reflected what I wanted and sharing my progress update with my therapist. The world around me wasn't really jumping for joy. Was this normal?

'You've been thinking about this for a long time,' she said. 'You've had a chance to get used to this new reality. They haven't. It's news to them. Give them a minute.'

Years later, speaking with a partner during a break-up, they gave the same response. 'You've had time to think about this – this is completely new and shocking to me.'

Gulp. Here I was feeling so smug about making those hard choices and I'd completely overlooked that awkward stage (because it IS awkward) of bringing people along for the ride or sharing my thinking with others. Did I really have to tell the whole world my inner workings? (Would their heads explode?)

But it makes sense, doesn't it?

Have you ever just needed a minute when someone told you something unexpected? Have you ever felt a pang of panic in your gut when someone you care about told you their plans to move jobs/countries/relationships? Have you ever felt shock when someone you love shared their dream to move further away from you? Have you ever felt in the dark and thought, 'Where the hell did this come from!?'

One reason people might have a hard time getting their head around your changes is simply because you have done work to get your head around them. You've reflected on what you need. You've created space for that to happen. You've created goals and dreams for yourself. Other people haven't rented time in your head to find out what's going on for you (thank goodness!). They mightn't have been aware of your thought processes. They have their own thoughts on their minds.

So, when you do share what you are moving away from and towards, don't be surprised if they aren't as excited as you – at first. This may be the first time they've heard what has been in your head for some time. And this doesn't mean they are rejecting you or poo-pooing the steps you are taking towards your own autonomy and growth.

No, they could be simply coming to terms with what this means for them.

Yep, them – not you! Now, this is when we start thinking about others and how they might be impacted by your growth.

Yep, everyone who isn't you is completely unaware of what you're thinking.

We are always, constantly, worrying about things from our own perspective, relative to our own comfort zones. This keeps us safe and is very normal. However, as we prepare to tell the world about the changes we've been making, the person we are speaking to is likely to be instinctively thinking, 'Hmm… what does this all mean for me?'

As you deliver your update, news or shift in focus, remember it is a new piece of information to people who aren't you, and they may not react the way you hope. This might happen if the change you are proposing means they see you less, or in a different capacity. A helpful way of being prepared for this is to give them the gift of some 'freak-out time'. That's right – expect pushback before they get their head around it. Know they're doing this as they're thinking about where they fit into your new life.

One expression of this is that they may ask you a lot of questions. This is actually a good sign. Instead of seeing these questions as criticisms, give yourself permission to think of them being asked because the other person really cares about you. They care about you so much that they are seeking clarity on what this means for you and for their relationship with you. They are seeking clarity so they can get on board with your new idea, change or life.

Help them understand your perspective. You might find it helpful to share with them how you were seeing things, and how these changes will help you feel happier in the long run.

Remember: any supportive person who wants the best for you will, over time, understand what's best for you.

However, some people may not accept your change, or may start acting up as a form of 'threat' or response to what you're sharing. You want to stick with the people whose reaction shifts from shock to support. But with those who stay in shock and refuse to accept your decisions, well... you'll have a case to create a boundary and insist that they respect it. If necessary, you'll need to enforce that boundary to create space between you and that person as you live your new life. (See Chapter 10 for how to communicate boundaries as you navigate a change.)

This might be really tough and take some time for you to wrap your head around. While you can be compassionate to a point, you can't always know what's going on for someone, so do be open to someone you care about not being okay with your next step.

As a result, you might find it helpful to mentally allocate 'freak-out credits' to those you share your evolution with. Some will use two or three credits, then eventually get on board. Others may move into double-digit territory. If so, that is a good prompter for you to reflect and ask where your line in the sand may be when it comes to choosing to share your life with that person or group of people. Obviously you will want to give people you care about the benefit of the doubt. Do remember: if you have to work that hard at keeping someone in your life, it mightn't be your life they're interested in.

Life is short. It's too short to be explaining yourself to people who don't want you to live your best life. You are too valuable and important to be dimming your light for anyone who isn't aboard Operation Happy and Fulfilled You. Give them the benefit of some time, but also allow a constructive balance between their shock and, eventually, support.

Some people might ghost you

As a result of the choices you are making and the new boundaries you have put into place, others might elect to step away from you without explanation. This is often called 'ghosting'.

I have people in my life who have chosen not to accept my choices and boundaries, and after much emotional turmoil between us both, I have never heard from them again. I could go crazy wondering why, or how, or what it means. Certainly, I've come close to it!

What I've learned is that, if someone puts space between you and them, they will have their reasons, and sometimes you'll never know what they are. As the saying goes, when people tell you who they are, believe them. I've come to learn that actions communicate plenty. If someone shows you who they are, take clues from their actions, not their words.

To grow, you'll need to figure out a way of being okay with that – or at least acknowledging and accepting what happened, even if you don't fully understand it.

It's likely you will still want closure for your own comfort. Of course you will. But in some instances, you will never be the wiser for why you haven't heard back from people. Unfortunately, they aren't your direct manager – it's not their job to give you feedback or a step-by-step diagram on how they feel and why. Their only job is to do the best they know how or what feels right to them. It is sad, and it can be hurtful. Be patient and kind to yourself during this process if you do experience this.

Some people may play the victim

Some people you love may also feel as if they are getting left behind because you are moving on. If you have been playing a protective, leadership, co-dependent or parental-type role in this relationship, this can add to an unhelpful dynamic.

Think about it. Even when you want the best for someone, it can come as a temporary shock when they move on in their professional or personal life. Instinctively, you will put a mirror up and ask, 'What does this mean about me/us?'

The same is true for those you share your news with. However, some will take it one step further and they'll play out a 'victim mindset' where things are happening 'to them' (and not you).

People who play the victim and put this emotional pressure on you often use exaggerated statements, such as:

- 'I can't believe you'd do this to me.'
- 'I need you.'
- 'You don't care about us anymore.'
- 'I can't believe you didn't think about me in this.'
- 'You never make time for me anymore.'
- 'Can't you see how this is impacting me?'
- 'I can't believe you'd do this when [personal tragedy unrelated to you] is happening.'
- 'You know I have a hard time with [unresolved personal trauma], so how could you do this to me?'
- 'Not since [traumatic event, could be from years ago] has someone done this to me.'

These statements are examples of what resilience experts refer to as an 'external locus of control' or 'victim mindset'. This means the person experiences life as events happening 'to' them, not around them. When someone has a victim mindset or an external locus of control, they believe life is a series of luck, fate or circumstances that they have no agency, autonomy or control over.

By contrast, and by choosing to take accountability for your life, you are choosing to utilise an 'internal locus of control'. This is the belief that you – YOU – are responsible for your own actions, behaviours and outcomes. You are not responsible for, and do not take responsibility for, things that happen to you or around you. You are only responsible for what you do next.

For this reason, at this stage of the process, many relationships and friendships can crack. As always, you have a choice. You can either choose to continue to enable their behaviour (this is often referred to as playing a 'rescuer' role), which keeps you both small and unhealthy, or you can choose to create a healthy boundary (an empowering role for both you and them).

Am I breaking up with a dynamic?

If someone you care about continues to play the victim, or their response does not transform from shock to support, you might be in a dynamic that psychologists call a 'dependency need'. Dependency needs in relationships can develop if someone does not feel safe, seen, respected or heard. In response, they can develop a dependency on having those needs fulfilled.

If you find yourself in this scenario, it may be that you have played a role in enabling this dependency in some way: for example, by offering financial aid, a listening ear, mental support, physical love or simply being available.

As a result, the other person may not have been in the habit of taking ownership. This is not your fault, but by playing a role, big or small, in enabling their behaviour over time, you have reinforced it in some way – perhaps by choosing to endorse it or simply looking the other way.

Where does dependency come from? A myriad of life experiences make us who we are, however when it comes to dependency, typically insecurity and fear can play a role, resulting in compounding inaction. As a result, they may have learned to lean on others to do the heavy lifting to get by. For example, instead of looking inward to build mental, physical, financial and emotional stability, they might seek their sense of security from your mental, physical, financial or emotional availability.

It's like looking for external validation. Gosh it feels good, but it isn't sustainable and doesn't come from a solid foundation of inner confidence.

As a result, unhelpful dynamics can develop.

If someone you care about has a dependency need, and you have in part been enabling that need, they might attempt to consistently talk you out of your personal growth by outlining how much they will be impacted. And if you are in the process of changing, that might be jarring to them.

You might experience this behaviour as needy, over-the-top, or perhaps even detached from reality. It can feel frustrating, annoying and tricky to extract yourself from a person who acts in this way when you are trying to show up as the person you want to be. This is particularly pertinent if you haven't enforced a boundary with this needy person in the past, even if you have discussed it in greater detail.

Action is a jolt to the person you're speaking to. It is firmly in the real world, and that can be daunting.

Remember, they are at the centre of this fear, not you. You are a tool in this dynamic, a tool to have their needs met. Remembering this can be helpful in looking at dynamics in new ways.

Don't be afraid to communicate your needs, and be open about what you would need in a different dynamic where you can both show up as your best. Exposure to your evolution could also give them confidence that if you can make change and navigate it as well as you have, well… maybe they can, too.

How to respond to others threatened by change

So, where to with this information? Here, you'll require a gentle but firm approach.

Jumping on a moral high horse will take the conversation to a very bad place very quickly. Remember, deciding to work on your growth doesn't make you superior or ahead of anyone else. It simply means you are making a choice to find what success means to you at this current moment in time. Everyone is doing life according to their own timeline and what is right for them.

I implore you to be your most patient, empathetic and compassionate self. Create the space and time (and it will take time) to hear the other person's reality. It might not reflect your reality, but make the time to hear how they see things.

As you do this, be sure to take mental note of what is your responsibility and what is no longer your responsibility. Talk to this other person who you still care about and share your genuine concern that by both of you continuing to have a dynamic that relies on one another, neither of you can grow.

If you find yourself becoming frustrated or tired, it will be hard to continue to treat the other person with kindness and respect. Try to go back to the time when you were first making the steps towards introspection, when you were questioning whether the habits, people and places of that time were helping you take your next step. Can you remember feelings of uncertainty and fear as you challenged yourself to enter your learning zone? When you first started to ask if there could be more, can you recall humbling moments of feeling like a total beginner as you embarked on this process? Recalling these moments can help you show up as your kinder self.

It can also help to remember that we miss people we love when they move on, and we want to be reassured that we will still play a role in their lives. Sometimes the person you're speaking to will simply want to know how they will be included in your next steps. Give yourself plenty of time to make room for creating space to hear them and share what a great dynamic could look like between you.

Self-reflection

Reflect on these questions if you find it tough to communicate firmly what you need:

What would a more balanced dynamic look like with a dependant person you care about?

What could a healthier relationship look like?

What boundaries could you put into place with this person to achieve this?

As you reflect on the questions in the exercise above, invite the person you care about to move to a different dynamic in which you are both enjoying your lives to the fullest. Acknowledge their fears, and gently remind them that this discussion is helping you both have a dynamic you can be proud of and that allows you both to live your best life in a sustainable way. Who wouldn't want that?

People may project their fears onto you

When you 'project' your feelings onto someone else, you make what that person shares with you about you and, commonly, your fears. Some experts say projection is a by-product of your ego's attempt to avoid uncertainty in life. It's like a defence mechanism you use to protect yourself against what you don't know. For example, you'd rather shut down an awesome idea than show uncertainty by asking more about it.

Research has discovered that there is a strong correlation between suppressing your fears and how you see the world. When you avoid self-awareness and self-discovery, you create a 'false reality' that simply reinforces your view. Why is this? Your brain loathes uncertainty. When you feel uncertain, you instinctively lean on defensiveness to protect yourself. Think about it: when you hear something you don't entirely understand, do you lean into curiosity, or judgement and dismissiveness? Typically the latter, I expect. This means your friends, colleagues and loved ones might be total assholes when they first hear your idea.

If you read my blogs and interviews, you might know I have referred to this as 'concern trolling'. It's projecting your fear onto someone else under the guise of 'just caring about that person'. It's passive aggression.

For example, typically when I say I work for myself, people are genuinely interested. They ask questions and want to know more, and are keen to learn about what that means to me, what inspires me and what I get out of having a different schedule each week. It's lovely to share how I feel with these people.

Others are a little less comfortable with the idea. They'll ask questions, but they phrase their questions in a way that make me feel I have to 'defend' my idea. I used to feel pretty strange about these interactions – until I realised I was being 'concern trolled'. I was being judged, passively aggressively, under the pretence of concern.

Being 'concern trolled'

Here's how you can tell if you are being asked questions out of genuine interest or whether you are getting concern trolled:

- The curiosity is false and the comments are 'backhanded'; for example, 'I'm just curious… why would you do that?' really means, 'Why on earth did you do that? What a terrible idea!'
- Any sentence that starts with 'don't you…' is typically a red flag; for example, 'Don't you worry about money/ getting clients?' really means, 'You're mad; you may not get clients or ever get paid.'
- They talk about their own reality; for example, 'I could never do that' really means, 'I'm far too smart to do that.'

Here are some examples of concern trolling in action (and these are all real-life examples):

'How was your morning?'
  'Great! I did a fitness class.'
'Oh, I could never do that sort of jumping around.'
    'Well, it's not for everyone, so…'
'Don't you worry about getting injured?

'Drink?'
    'I'm good thanks.'
'Sure I can't get you something to drink?'
    'Sure – mineral water?'
'Don't you drink? I don't drink that much. I'm giving up drinking next week.'

'So, what do you do?'
    'I run my own business. How about you?'
'Oh, I could never work for myself. Isn't it really hard?'
(Classic projection.)

The gift of active listening

When you are on the receiving end of this style of communication, it can be tempting to shrug and move on. Remember, when someone projects, they aren't poo-pooing your idea: they are simply responding out loud to how they'd approach your scenario.

Active listening is when you listen without applying your perspective or point of view to the other person's idea. You listen without judgement. The reason we teach courses on this, and why it's so popular in leadership, is because learning how to actually listen to absorb other people's content (instead of waiting to talk!) often takes a serious dose of relearning, or 'unlearning' old habits.

In these moments, if you are on the receiving end of projection or what feels like negative enquiry, it can be helpful to use clarifying statements. These statements help you separate what the person is projecting towards you and what their fears could include from your experience and your reality. It's helpful both for setting boundaries and in managing expectations (in work and life) – a powerful tool to separate emotion from facts.

Clarifying statements can help you put subtle boundaries in place with minimal freak-out effects on the other party. Here's what you can do:

- Try clarifying the question before choosing to respond. You can do this by reverse-engineering your answer to seek understanding of what they are truly curious about. For example, when they say, 'Don't you…' you can ask, 'Do you?' or, 'Is that top of mind for you when thinking about X?' This can help them reflect on what they are truly curious about or inspire them to divulge what comes up for them as they hear what you're talking about. And you can gain greater understanding of their point of view and replace any internal disappointment you may have with curiosity.

- If you're feeling judged, tease them with, 'Are you judging me right now?' Incredulousness can snap people out of their own ridiculousness, I have discovered! It also lightens the mood.

- Share how it makes you feel. In one instance with someone I care about very deeply, I opted to tell them that their negativity stopped me from sharing my news with them; it made it hard for me to connect with them. Over time, this made a huge difference to understanding each other's point of view.

- You may find it helpful to remember you have the option to move on and change the topic if you aren't emotionally invested in the person you're speaking to understanding you fully or being 'fully briefed' on your next step. Sometimes a headline is all you need to land. If others do opt to share their negativity, well… let them! If you are comfortable not feeding it, you can simply move on and change the subject.

Chapter 10

CREATING HELPFUL DEFENCE MECHANISMS

Now that you are aware of how some people will react to your personal growth and the changes you have been making, you probably agree that you'll need some defence mechanisms to keep you going in difficult times. These are an important part of your survival guide.

Creating healthy boundaries

Get ready for your life to change! Creating boundaries is an essential way to get more of what you want.

What are boundaries? Boundaries are tools for communicating your needs. As we discussed in Chapter 9, this doesn't always come naturally. Sometimes, we need some help getting there as our confidence grows in this area.

Learning how to say no will change your life

How do you communicate your boundaries? A great place to start is learning how to say no to things you don't want to do, or things you do want to do but that don't serve you anymore. An effective tool many of my clients use is the No Sandwich. Here's how it works.

Validate the request

We all crave validation and seek to feel heard. Validation is an appreciation and acknowledgement tool you can use to achieve this. In one study comparing conversational dynamics where validation was used, it was discovered that the moods of participants who had been validated were restored following the interaction. Invalidated participants' moods got worse! To validate someone asking if you can come to dinner, or help on a project, or borrow some money, you can say any number of positively framed statements that focus on appreciation for their time. Here are some examples:

- 'I appreciate you thinking of me.'
- 'Thanks for asking.'
- 'I can see why you might think that.'
- 'That's a common misconception.'
- 'Thanks for the invite!'
- 'Ordinarily I would be keen and free.'

At the minimum, it's about acknowledgement. Rightly or wrongly, the person asking feels it is a valid question, so resist the temptation to baulk at their request and instead acknowledge them so that, at a minimum, they feel heard.

Say no

The trick to saying no is to not make it personal. Remember: they're asking you because you usually say yes. This exercise is part education, part managing expectations. Here are some examples:

- 'I can't make it.'
- 'I don't do that anymore.'

- 'I'm focusing on other things these days.'
- 'This isn't for me.'
- 'This isn't a fit.'
- 'I'm at capacity right now.'

At this juncture it can be helpful to remember 'no' is also a full sentence!

When you are in a close relationship, you can be even more direct to help those you care about know what you're more interested in. Here are some examples:

- 'To be honest, those movies aren't really my jam anymore. I'm more into X these days…'
- 'Honestly? I'm so slammed this week. I just need a night to myself under my blanket.'
- 'I need some down time this week. Raincheck?'
- 'No time this week unfortunately!'

Suggest another pathway to have the request fulfilled

If it's a 'no, but under different circumstances…', this is a wonderful way to communicate your needs gently and educate the person on what you need to be able to say yes:

- 'Sunday is out for me, but how about Wednesday?'
- 'I don't do that during work hours, but how about next weekend?'
- 'I'm at capacity this week, how about in a few weeks time? Say, X?'
- 'I'm on deadlines this week! Let me come back to you.'
- 'I usually can, but this week I'm out. Have fun, and see you next time.'

- 'I don't hang out with that crew anymore, but I'd love to catch up with you. If you're keen, we could grab a coffee in a different part of town?'
- 'I need some space from that right now. I'll give you a text in a few weeks and we can touch base then.'

See, you can get really creative here! Texts, calls back and emails can give you plenty of time to think about communicating what it is that you need before you respond. The main thing with communicating boundaries successfully is being unapologetically clear. Being clear helps the other person understand what you need. If being direct is a new step for you, you can practise your responses until you find a catchphrase that works best for you.

In a work situation, I strongly recommend you opt to educate the person asking where they can find an answer to their enquiry. In working relationships, collaboration is critical, and simply diverting the person's query in the direction of someone who can help them is a great way to develop trustworthy, respectful relationships in which you demonstrate you are invested in their success. A few simple suggestions can help the other person take a sensible next step. Here are a few examples:

- 'I don't do that anymore, but the X department can help you with that. The person to speak to is X.'
- 'I used to do X, and now Y person looks after that. Do you need their details?' Or, 'They are CCed here.'
- 'I can help you in two weeks. If you need it sooner than then, and I appreciate you might do, I recommend speaking to Y, or connecting with my manager to review priorities.'

- 'My area of expertise is X, and it seems you might be supported by a Y person. I've listed a few people in my network who may be a good fit for you. Good luck!'

You don't need to respond right away

One example of feeling uncomfortable communicating your needs is if you often feel 'put on the spot' or in your panic zone when people ask you a question. My clients have found a stepping stone to creating helpful boundaries in techniques to buy themselves time to figure out what they might say and how they might say it. Buying yourself time in interactions is a helpful way to stop and allow yourself to think clearly, and get yourself back into your learning or comfort zone.

Confident communication from a strong sense of self benefits everyone around you. When you feel put on the spot, you are more likely to say yes to meetings you don't need to attend, say things you don't mean or communicate indirectly and unhelpfully. If you work in a 'reactive' culture, chances are your peers are feeling put on the spot, too.

Here are some examples of how you can create space to give yourself time to reflect on what your needs are and decide whether you want to say yes or no. At work, you can ask for requests in writing, and outside of work you can be open about needing to check your schedule or review all the details before making a decision.

- 'Let me think about that and come back to you.'
- 'Ordinarily I'd say yes right away, but I've got a few things on, so I'll let you know as soon as I can.'
- 'Good question. Let me check my schedule and I'll loop back.'

THERE HAS TO BE MORE

- 'I'll have a think about that. It sounds good, but I'll need to check some details before I say yes.'
- 'Sounds interesting! Send me an email with your thoughts mapped out and an overview?'
- 'I can't commit right away, so I'll circle back.'
- 'I'd love to think about it. Can you tell me a little more?'
- 'Can't chat right now! Talk next week?'

The main rule is that you never need to commit on the spot. Unless you're in a life-or-death scenario.

When pressure is applied

When you first start to communicate your boundaries, you may encounter some resistance and pushback. Sometimes this might be the other person being in the habit of you always saying yes, and them, of course, benefitting from that.

Psychologist Nedra Glover Tawwab's work demonstrates that there are two parts to enforcing boundaries. The first is communicating our needs. The second is enforcing them. Enforcing our boundaries becomes incredibly important when it comes to other people respecting them. If you experience this breaking down at work, it's typically because of poor planning. I see this a lot in project-based work, where one person, either through poor planning skills or lack of support, causes a destructive flow-on effect through panic and last-minute decision-making. This is exacerbated when working with colleagues who have poor communication techniques and low emotional regulation, and who work within hierarchical structures (erm... see why it's so common?)

When I am on the receiving end of this, this is a helpful phrase I like to remember: 'someone else's lack of planning does not make it my emergency.' I need to remind myself to stay strong with my boundaries by ensuring I enforce a consequence of my needs.

When pressure is applied, it can be helpful to document your needs and requests, and have them nearby (at least in the short term as you build the habit of communicating your needs). Here are some practical techniques I have used to great effect to help me maintain and enforce boundaries in life and work as I grew my confidence in this area:

- I put boundaries in my diary by blocking out what my intention for the day is. That might include a client task, being with family or simply having a mental day off. I am (now) in the routine of checking my diary when I am asked for favours and referring to that before saying yes or no. I know I don't have to extend my imagination to come up with a tangible lie – I'm acting with integrity by doing what I intend to on certain days, and I can be as transparent about it as I feel like.

- I now ask for help in advance of when I need it. As an example, when I'm asked to help with child care and I'm not available, or I've promised to do something in particular (even if just to myself), I can protect myself from my genuine urge to say yes by checking my calendar. If I have to say no, I suggest one or two other people who could potentially help out (that I've checked earlier are okay for me to suggest). My compassion is tempered with the knowledge there are other resources out there. I am not the 'only' person who can help, I remind myself.

- I am now in the habit of asking whether I need to be the person who solves the problem. As my level of decision-making increases, so does my fatigue and ability to make thoughtful decisions. I have started to think about my mental energy as a finite resource to spread evenly across the day. If I am tempted to solve a problem, I now ask, 'Is this my problem to solve?' This helps me maintain a healthy boundary between what is and isn't my job or business!

- I don't check emails or Slack within certain hours as I know I will be tempted to help with problems that can be solved by others. I protect myself from my habit to help!

- I block my calendar by task to ensure I don't extend my boundaries to help people who aren't on my day's focus or priority list. Each night, I review: 'Did I get my most important thing done? If not, why not? What did I reprioritise? Why? What would I do differently, if anything?' This reflection exercise helps me grow my boundaries, confidence and habit every day.

- I ask my team to report outcomes to me each week and share that I expect they come with a list to discuss. To support this, I purposefully don't review their to-do list; instead I focus on what clarification I require for them. As a result, if they forget, I can reassert that they need to prepare to have a productive connection. I am also less tempted to go through their list as I simply don't have it!

- I ask if people have read the pre-meeting materials. If they haven't, I have been known to reschedule meetings to send the message: come prepared. (I think I needed about a week to recover from communicating that boundary.)

- I test my understanding to check scope with clients if and when the project evolves. Saying things such as, 'My understanding of what we're here to do is X, and it seems we are talking about Y. Would we agree that's a separate project?' helps me clarify the scope while also acknowledging the desire to work on other projects.

- When I find myself offering to pay, as is my nature, I've trained myself to pause at the cash register when with others so we all get our wallets out at the same time – a small hack that has helped my generosity to come from a place of equity.

As you can see, maintaining your boundaries is a personal endeavour that can benefit every element of your life. Commitment to protecting yourself from yourself, or from your defaults, is a small, helpful step towards getting increasingly confident communicating your needs and what you want more of.

Managing your frustration

In Chapter 8, we talked about feeling resentful of people you love – particularly if they have not given you the support you had hoped for. Sometimes this resentment may develop into feelings of anger. If this happens, I urge you to ask yourself this: 'Is it possible I feel hurt, devastated, embarrassed, shocked, surprised or disappointed in this moment? Did I expect person X to respond differently? Or did they meet my expectations and I hoped for something different? What was it that caused my hurt?'

And for those of you who are ready to take it one step further, think about at what point you were able to translate that hurt into anger.

If anger is your default response when you feel hurt – and it is for many people who have not felt safe or supported in their life from people who should have known better – it might be tempting to blame them and talk about them to others.

This may help you to digest the feelings and work through them in the short term, but believe me, leaving a barrage of text messages, long emails and voicemails outlining your feelings will not help in the long term. I know plenty of clients and peers who have turned to alcohol, drugs and partying as a way to experience peace during times of hurt and processing. If this self-destruction is tempting, you are certainly not alone.

The tale of the missing employee

In one example, I coached an employee who was showing up inconsistently at work. 'They're a total superstar at work for six months, then... something happens and I don't hear from them for days,' said their boss. 'They're such a star, I'd love to support them and identify how we can help.' Could I help?

In our one-on-one, the employee and I reflected on ways that self-sabotage (a fear of success) can see us finding ways to break things around us, such as trusted relationships or a great track record at work. In this instance, when work got hard, they went on an alcohol bender. Alcohol was their drug of choice, but the pain point was their relationship to responsibility and the hard things that come with taking accountability, such as important conversations, delegation and managing energy levels as a leader.

Over time, and through reflection, this team member was able to have a dialogue with their boss, and while I'm certain they didn't share the exact details of why they went missing for days, they were able to have an honest dialogue around expectations. Together they were able to discuss what success looked like, and the employee agreed that they could be called out on the pattern when it emerged.

So rarely do we even stop to reflect on how our behaviour causes a flow-on effect to everyone around us. All of this time got taken up from a place of fear of responsibility, which turned into frustration and anger, and all of a sudden your boss is calling Rachel Service.

That's where coaching, using tools of self-reflection to create self-empowerment, can really change the game. I can tell you that from first-hand experience.

Create ways to let it go

Speaking of anger, there is absolutely a time and a place for getting together with people who love and care about you to say, 'Fuck them! Fuck that person!' I have certainly found that incredibly cathartic myself. I remember once, after a break-up, taking my 'memory box' of photos and artefacts to a close friend's house and ceremoniously putting it into a tin and setting it on fire. Gosh, it felt good. Real good.

But...

After that, there was no going back – which is why I had avoided burning the darn box of photos in the first place, because it meant I would have to move on. I'd have to step into ambiguity that I knew would technically be good for me but would require me to change, to grow up a bit.

And this is exactly why so many people don't lean into the process of letting go – not because they don't want to, but rather because it means they are no longer choosing to connect to that person. And this brings its own type of grief.

Even if the person you are separating yourself from is not right to accompany you on your journey through the Growth Cycle to the new you, you can't deny the genuine care you may still have for them in some way. Even if they've been really sub-par as a human to you, or treated you unkindly or ungratefully, you get comfortable with what you know.

If you've ever gone back to a relationship after a break-up with a person who you knew was not good for you – and, as I have done, hidden it from your friends – you'll know the big-time temptation not to cut those ties.

However, there was a reason I hid this from my friends: because, deep down, I knew this was not good for me and didn't reflect where I was really going. I had faith that I could do better. There was this little voice inside of me saying, 'Rach, this isn't it. There is more out there! Go out and get it!'

So, you must urge yourself to find the courage to finish the work you started. A pep talk with the 'best' you – your biggest, most powerful future self – is necessary.

And part of this is a process of letting go. You'll need to draw a line in the sand to separate where you have been from where you are going.

If you choose not to – and all action is a choice, remember – the hurt will creep into all the hard work you've done to date. You will experience a breach in your personal integrity. You will do things at odds with what you truly believe in or propose to believe in.

There is resounding evidence to suggest that our brains mostly function on autopilot and that our beliefs, thoughts and habits are driven by our subconscious. So, don't be mad that your default might be rage. I urge you not to accept that anger is your only choice. You always have a choice. With conscious practice, setting boundaries and showing compassion, I promise it is possible to override rage with something more productive for your sanity and that of those around you.

As someone who is invested in your success, I take you seriously and, consequently, I urge you to take this seriously. You are better than a short-temper tantrum. Find a place to let it out safely, then let it go. Non-team sports, weightlifting, high-intensity exercise and professional therapists, counsellors or coaches are great places to start.

Distancing yourself

Sometimes, while we can feel disappointed, we are not always surprised by how others respond to our exciting news.

If this is your experience and you are on the receiving end of unhelpful communication, it can be helpful to reflect on whether you had any prior evidence of that person responding differently to similar circumstances.

Was the reason you had hoped for a different outcome based on experience or hope?

I remember feeling frustrated and exhausted, and explaining this to my doctor. It wasn't until I spent a few sessions with a deeply compassionate and helpful therapist that I began to understand. I was still mad at myself and others for not knowing how to put boundaries in place! Grumble grumble.

And I was holding on, subconsciously, to that feeling. It was following me everywhere without my knowing, and as a result I was feeling frustrated and fed up.

Frustration was the symptom, but the real rock in my way was my inability to communicate my needs and let go of how other people responded to those new expectations.

At this juncture, I want to ask you if you expect the person you harbour frustration towards to give you anything. This is a really important step as it helps you hone in on what is really causing you to be uncomfortable.

Self-reflection

With regard to the person you are holding anger towards, ask yourself:

Do I feel this person 'owes' me something *(for example, an apology)*?

_____

_____

_____

_____

Am I expecting someone to deliver closure for me *(for example, context as to why, signs of regret or remorse)*?

_____

_____

_____

Am I expecting anything in return for my growth or boundary *(for example, a simple thank you)*?

_____

_____

_____

What could letting go of expectation look like or feel like *(for example, not expecting a response, being okay if I don't hear back, them responding as I do expect!)*?

_____

_____

_____

Oof. This has often been a real shocker for some of my clients, and certainly I've wrestled with these questions myself in the past. The reason this reflection is so important is that it highlights what so many of us don't like to admit: our growth and mental freedom are not contingent on what someone else does or says. They rely on us to focus only on what we can control ourselves.

If you find yourself in this situation, it's best to remember the person you are thinking about doesn't actually owe you anything. This might hurt to hear. But they don't.

It's your job to understand your feelings and communicate your needs. It's not their job to reconcile your hurt, or even to own up to what may have caused you distress. You might be getting a bit pissed off reading that, especially if anger is your immediate expression of hurt. 'Why the hell not?' I hear you say.

Well, you're the one who has changed. You're the one who has inserted the boundary. It wasn't working for you. It may have been working for them. (Remember, you may have been a tool to fulfil a need in many unhelpful dynamics.)

If this person chooses to reject your boundary, avoid you, ghost you or respond in any way that doesn't suit you, they don't actually need to say sorry.

You might feel like they should. But you are the one who gets to decide what standard you accept as the entry fee for playing a role in your life. You get to decide if their behaviour is up to your standards. You can put a boundary in place, but you can't demand someone apologises for behaviour that actually suits them.

I know that is crappy and unfair and uncomfortable and, in some scenarios, ethically or legally upside-down. I know. But the deal you made with yourself, in pursuit of growth, was to pursue a life of peace of mind – for you, not for anyone else.

If you are feeling angry, it can be empowering to outline how you could create your own way of giving yourself peace in that particular moment. I am not asking you to ignore justice. I am simply asking you to reflect on what path of action will give you peace and fulfilment. Wishing someone will 'get what they deserve' gives away your power and causes you to look to the past instead of the future. This sucks up valuable headspace and time you could spend living the life you're working towards.

Wishing others harm stops you from letting go. It makes your happiness contingent on their suffering. This is not growth. It connects you to them. It is the antithesis of letting go. Wishing harm on others is petty and keeps you small. Wishing someone nothing at all is quite the boss move. Once you've experienced that, you can start to cultivate feelings of gratitude for their role in your life and, eventually, send them no ill will at all.

Validating your thoughts

One of the most powerful steps to making sense of your past and circumstances you don't understand is to have someone validate your thoughts and actions, to help you see your perspective as just one part of the puzzle.

You might opt to do this with a supportive friend or loved one, and I certainly endorse seeing a counsellor, coach or trained professional who can help you with this process.

Once you have had a chance to digest the pain someone has caused you, my advice is to let them be, wish them no harm and move on with your life. That way, if you bump into them in the future, you have not wasted negative energy sending them bad vibes and will be less likely to blurt out any deeply harboured rage out of shock. If instead you have harboured pain, anger or blame towards them, and have not taken the steps to unpack and feel those emotions in a safe space, it will 100 per cent find a way to play out later in your life, and as I outlined earlier in the book, your body or subconscious will find a way to replay that drama in future through psychosomatic symptoms or seeing life through a red-filtered lens. You can't underplay the role of unprocessed emotions and how they might affect you.

It is also likely that your next relationship (romantic or platonic) will hear all about this drama, which is a major turnoff. (I know this from personal experience!)

In summary, nothing ends well when you harbour rage.

Let it go by finding a safe space to process and accept the actions of others, so you can continue taking control of your emotional regulation to achieve what you want out of life. You are better than this moment right now.

Saying goodbye to some people

At some stage during this process, it may become clear that some people in your life are not the right fit for where you are going or who you have become. There are practical steps you can take to have open and honest conversations with the people you care about.

As an outcome of these conversations, you might decide to put a boundary in place, create space between you or say goodbye entirely. This does not mean you have failed, or that you are leaving people behind. What this does mean is that, if you have communicated your needs and intentions and those you care about cannot support you, you might need to make a choice to go forward without their support.

If you do decide to do this, know that there are a number of resources available to you, listed at the end of this book, that you can call upon to help you navigate that change.

Chapter 11

KICKING DOUBT TO THE KERB

Reading about the Growth Cycle might have you thinking, 'Geez, this is a bit of work.' I understand. Particularly if you are new to the process of investing in your own development, this might feel a bit daunting or overwhelming. I get it.

But the truth is that awesome lives don't just appear out of nowhere. They are cultivated over time. Boundaries are set. Needs are communicated. Expectations evolve. Wants are shared. Precedents are created. Views are expressed. What you tolerate changes.

Just as you change, the people you care for change and the world changes. What you used to say yes to, you might not want to anymore. What used to suit you might have outgrown its benefit. The people in your life may have made different lifestyle choices that aren't reflecting your current or future reality.

To enjoy your life, sometimes you have to do hard things. In this section, I show you techniques to help you manage self-doubt as you go through the process.

Managing your inner perfectionist

During my first burnout, I moved back into my parents' house. They kindly rearranged their lives to accommodate their twenty-something-year-old, burnt-out daughter, who had been recently diagnosed with depression and anxiety, living back in her childhood bedroom.

My parents, with the support of professionals, supervised me with grace and compassion to make sure I was eating, sleeping and not overworking until I was well enough to go back to work and move out of home again. It was an extremely humbling experience, and I am eternally grateful for their love and example.

As part of my recovery, I attempted to create habits and routines around my new identity of being burnt out. One of these habits was a daily run.

On the day of my first attempt, I walked to the end of the driveway and… I couldn't do it. I could barely move my legs further than the house. I felt simultaneously overwhelmed, exhausted and paralysed. I slowly walked back to the house feeling defeated.

My dad arrived home that evening. 'How was your day, Rach?'

I shrugged. 'I couldn't even go for a run. I got to the driveway and had to go back.'

He smiled. 'To the driveway! Well, that is fantastic. You know Rach, something is better than nothing.'

And I've never forgotten it. In fact, I often say to myself at the end of a day when I felt I could have done something more, 'Something is better than nothing.'

It sounds counterintuitive for a recovering perfectionist, but what my dad taught me is something called 'positive reframing'. Psychologists have found this to be the link between healthy perfectionism and perfectionism that stops you from taking helpful action.

Two types of perfectionism

There are two types of perfectionism: adaptive and maladaptive. Both adaptive and maladaptive perfectionists share the desire for high standards and the pursuit of excellence.

Adaptive perfectionists are aware of their strengths and have a pragmatic relationship with their weaknesses. They are more readily able to adapt to things not going to plan. They are able to say 'something is better than nothing' when they don't meet their own expectations.

In contrast, maladaptive perfectionists experience high stress when the standards they set for themselves and others are not met. Rather than adapting their expectations, small hiccups or alterations to plans can cause them great distress and frustration. In fact, studies have discovered a link between maladaptive perfectionism and burnout. In one analysis of multiple studies on the topic, it was discovered that athletes, students and employees who demonstrated signs of maladaptive perfectionism experienced more burnout. In my example of going for a run, I was exhibiting signs of both burnout and maladaptive perfectionism. I was beating myself up while I was down and, as a result, I was suffering and unable to see the bigger picture or give myself compassion in a moment when it would have aided my experience and confidence.

It's been said that the pursuit of perfection, or a perfect life, is not the pursuit of the best in ourselves but of the worst in ourselves.

If you want to throw in the towel if something is not 'perfect' or 'right' the first time, you might be experiencing symptoms of maladaptive perfectionism. From my own experiences and working with hundreds of clients who have shared the same thought pattern, I can promise you it is possible to rewire your brain. It will take work, but it is possible to utilise what makes you driven and repurpose it for a compassionate existence compatible with a life of growth.

Perfectionists seeking support to grow, in my experience, want to know how not to fail before they begin. They read as much as they can before taking any action to ensure they do it perfectly. This is to avoid feelings of embarrassment or disappointing others by 'letting others down'.

Where does this come from? I am no psychoanalyst, but my work has given me plenty of case studies to draw upon. Some of my clients who demonstrate maladaptive perfectionist traits have shared with me that they believe they only receive love, or are worthy of recognition from parental figures, if they do something to the highest possible standard. Others shared experiences of being with narcissists and feeling paralysed when seeking to take action for fear of being criticised or being taken advantage of. Others felt they were only noticed if they did 'the most'. As a result, they cultivated expressions of perfectionism through work, how they dressed and how they communicated with others.

Unsupported perfectionists, in my experience, are both brilliant (as they have high expectations of themselves) and a challenge to work alongside or have on your team (as they require constant validation and reassurance they are good enough, and will even miss deadlines or submit partly finished work for feedback to avoid submitting in its entirety and receiving a critique). Perfectionists can also have a tough time growing in the presence of others, preferring to fail privately in the safety of a 'judgement-free' zone.

While perfectionism can be a driver of excellence, it can also be an inhibitor if not channelled towards taking small steps of positive action. Maladaptive perfectionists also avoid taking action, preferring to remind themselves of what could go wrong.

The commonality all perfectionists share is self-critique. The difference between adaptive and maladaptive perfectionists, though, is how they manage this self talk and, as a result, mentally manage experiences.

Showing self-compassion

There is no magic pill you can take to not be a perfectionist anymore, and I wouldn't want you to minimise what makes you unique and brilliant. But there is something you can do every day to shift from maladaptive to adaptive pursuits of excellence so you can use your perfectionism to drive your happiness.

Studies have shown that self-compassion bridges the gap between perfectionism and constructive thoughts and actions. Developing a practice of checking in with yourself regularly and replacing negative thoughts with positive thoughts slowly, over time, rewires your thought patterns to default to accepting and compassionate thinking. You can do this by creating a safe space in your daily thoughts. One way to do this is to replace thinking about what you could lose with what you could gain. This doesn't undermine your valid concerns; it simply reframes your thoughts positively from a worst-case scenario to a best-case scenario to give you a wider scope of focus (as opposed to a purely negative view).

This is something I do in almost every class I teach when encouraging people to try something new for the first time. Reflecting on what you could gain ahead of a new situation helps people build greater confidence in taking small actions. Moving away from self-judgement and towards curiosity provides a helpful frame for thinking.

Table 5 lists some examples my coaching clients have given me, which may give you some ideas.

Table 5: Showing self-compassion

Before (judgement)	After (curiosity)
'I hate public speaking.'	'I'm trying something outside my comfort zone.'
'I'm nervous about what my boss will think.'	'I wonder what feedback will help me improve.'
'It's not perfect.'	'It's a start, which is better than nothing.'
'I won't know anything.'	'I don't know what I don't know.'
'Of course I'd muck it up.'	'I'm going to reflect on what I could do differently next time.'
'You're so stupid.'	'You're trying.'
'It'll be shit.'	'I have to start somewhere.'

You can cultivate empowerment in your daily life, every day, by talking to yourself from a place of compassion, just as you would expect a trusted friend or loved one to speak to you, or you to speak to someone you love and care about deeply.

Another way you can encourage your inner perfectionist to drive you forward is to make it safe to extend yourself through small, low-risk steps that can be hugely beneficial. Identifying ways to celebrate 'small wins' can contribute to confidence and resilience, and improve your ability to ask for help to manage nuanced situations. Researchers refer to this as the 'progress principle': the idea that if we feel we are making progress towards our goals, or some form of progression, we have a greater experience of satisfaction.

I have discussed defining your version of success as well as creating your definition of failure, and it's this sentiment I encourage you to remind yourself of if and when you find you are giving yourself a hard time during this process. Does failure really mean X not being done to perfection, or does failure simply mean not trying at all?

For those of you wondering, I started running again the very next day. It wasn't far, but it was something. And that something was the start of celebrating small wins and mirroring the compassionate role models around me.

Managing your inner critic

How do you counter negative talk when it's you who's doing the talking? By focusing on what you have to gain rather than lose, and by surrounding yourself with a positive support team, you can reframe self-criticism as a compassionate cheerleader.

Firstly, negative self-talk is something we learn from our environment. The combined effects of our upbringing, the people we surround ourselves with, expectations (real and imagined), our learnings and perceived failures – plus tall poppy syndrome, common in Australia and New Zealand, which puts people down when they achieve things – mean we often become who we need to be just to ensure our needs of social survival are met.

THERE HAS TO BE MORE

Self-criticism is a learned, and sometimes rewarded, behaviour. If people in our network also have a negative mindset, we are more likely to be self-critical. The inner critic thrives on feedback from those who do not want us to be successful. To overcome this, we must seek validation from those we respect who want us to succeed.

While self-talk is a result of your exposure, it is absolutely within your control and your responsibility to reframe those thoughts to create a different reality for your future.

We don't abolish negative thoughts: instead, we replace them. We never 'rid' ourselves of our inner critic. Rather, we build new thought processes to manage these thoughts when they arise. Taking the time to gain clarity on what you want and build your self-confidence through this book is a huge step in and of itself.

Coping with impostor syndrome

Impostor syndrome is a phenomenon where, despite all evidence to the contrary, you are convinced you are about to be exposed as a fraud and do not deserve the success you have achieved. You dismiss any proof of success as luck, timing or a result of tricking others into thinking you're better than you really are.

If you feel like this, it might be reassuring to know that 70 per cent of people report feeling like an 'impostor' at some point in their careers. These include Academy Award–winning actress Viola Davis, author and former First Lady of the United States Michelle Obama and billionaire and CEO Mike Cannon-Brookes.

There will never be a time you wake up and say, 'I am ready. I'm qualified enough. I'm the best in my field.' As comedian

Amy Poehler says, 'You will never climb Career Mountain and get to the top and shout, "I made it!"' However, there are a number of tools you can use to support your mindset as you stretch outside your comfort zone.

The antidote to imposter syndrome is confidence, which comes from a mix of evidence, validation and self-belief (as I outlined in Chapter 2). These three elements, when consistently built and reiterated, have helped hundreds of my clients manage feelings of impostor syndrome and replace unhelpful thoughts with new thoughts that drive them forward.

Symptoms of impostor syndrome can show up when your self-belief is tested or you are branching out into new territories. Elements of self-doubt can be incredibly adhesive when you are evolving or shifting your relationship with your identity. Your relationship with your self-esteem is being reimagined based on new criteria. How you see yourself, and how you see yourself living your life, is evolving.

Confidence, self-worth and self-belief will always get you to where you want to go. You are only limited by your perception of what you deserve, a lack of clarity as to what you really want and self-belief that you can pull it off.

Below, I outline four ways to overcome negative self-talk and feelings of impostor syndrome:

1. **Show compassion to yourself first.** Negative self-talk thrives on perceived failures. To show compassion to others, you must first show it to yourself. You are deserving of success on your own terms. See Chapter 9 for examples of moving from judgement to curiosity to develop this mental muscle.

2. **Articulate your achievements with an Achievement Audit.** Writing down your achievements, reviewing them and sharing them with those who want you to succeed can help quieten your inner critic. This is validation based in fact, not thought. See Chapter 2, which discusses this exercise in detail.

3. **Reframe negative thoughts.** Actively reframing your thoughts helps immensely. A Harvard Business Review study found people who reframed 'I'm nervous' to 'I'm excited' performed better at maths tests, public speaking and even karaoke. Why? Anxiety and excitement are both states of arousal, and reframing a fear into an action helps to take positive action. See Chapter 1 for examples of this.

4. **Cultivate a network of supporters, not critics.** Validation from people who want you to succeed is one of the quickest ways to remove roadblocks to your growth. Creating a network of people who want to support you, teach you, help you learn and see you succeed will enable you to voice any thoughts and have them validated by supporters who want to help you grow. Be sure to seek feedback and advice from people who have done what you are looking to achieve, or who you have respect for, as opposed to those who simply have an opinion or share proximity with you. People can be very helpful when you pose a question in a way that demonstrates respect and a willingness to learn. See Chapter 7 for the People Audit tool, which can help you cultivate a great network that reflects your future steps.

Fear is a temporary emotion

Biologically, your brain was created to keep you safe, and you are doing something brave: taking yourself out of your comfort zone to build a life that reflects who you are and who you are becoming. You know now when your comfort zone is having a tantrum that you're taking yourself into the learning zone.

As a part of this, it's normal if you hear your mind making comfortable excuses or reasons for this process not to work. You and I both know that's your panic zone settling in. The most important thing is that you don't let that feeling create a permanent home in your mind.

Remember, you are designing a life around your strengths. You are making decisions that suit your default, not someone else's. You are creating a life that suits you. This entire exercise is about taking control of your career, your relationships and your happiness. Is it helping you live a life that suits you? Or is it reflective of someone else's version of success?

It can be scary prioritising yourself. Sometimes it's confidence, sometimes it's fear, and sometimes it's simply about creating a new identity for yourself. The great news is that all transformation, good and bad, starts with a decision to endorse a certain type of behaviour. And you have control over how you choose to operate your life.

To paraphrase Beyoncé, when you're not feeling your best, you can ask yourself this: what am I going to do about it? How can I use negativity to fuel a transformation into a better me?

Our lives are all built on what we choose to do once we realise we want something different to what we currently have.

Your life is a direct reflection of what you prioritise. I urge you to prioritise yourself and invite yourself in for a really rewarding and empowering experience. The payoff is excellent, trust me.

When something doesn't work out

You've accepted that there has to be more. You've told your network about your growth journey. You've updated your LinkedIn. You've taken a new job, or said yes to a new relationship, or debuted a new outfit, or launched a new venture. You've had hard conversations. You've gotten your family and friends onboard.

And there's a hitch. The job falls through. The new person in your life is not who you thought they were. The workplace is nothing like what you had in mind. Your first client cancels. You start to feel lonely. It's financially tough. You hate your new house.

It will be very tempting to want to press 'undo' and revert to your previous life choices. This is your old identity calling and wanting to cash in. It wants you to return to your old comfort zone; it wants the old you! And it will work hard to lure you back in, believe me.

NO! No! Do not take a step back. Instead, pause to remind yourself of the bigger perspective. Stay with me here.

Do you remember the section of the Growth Cycle where you outlined your version of success? Get that out – it's in Chapter 6. Now is the time to remind yourself of your version of success. What does it say? Can you remind yourself of the reason you opted to make a change in the first place?

Your success does not ride on what is happening right now but on what you say, think and do next. It may be very tempting to quit. But you have a chance to create a new pattern in your life. You can make different choices knowing what you know now.

I want to also remind you of the choices you made around what you decided to compromise on in Chapter 6. Go back and review those. If you have followed the Growth Cycle, you have already made a decision about what you will accept and what you will compromise on.

You might simply be having that belief tested for the first time if something is not going to plan. The good news is that you have a chance to catch yourself and remind your old identity that the new identity has a new definition of success. By now, you know that real change happens when you make time to think, get serious about what you want, decide what you're willing to compromise on and then take small steps of action. And you get to cash in your hard work right now. This is the time you get to grow your confidence by taking one more step forward.

You might be tempted to quit, especially if the people around you are still coming to terms with your new life choices. I understand very well the gravitational pull of a failed expectation and wanting to throw in the towel. In fact, I have a conversation just like this with myself about once a year. The urge is strong, however it is only when things get hard. I have a choice to get back up again, and when I do, my work, my confidence, my self-esteem and, consequently, my business get stronger.

I hope it is helpful to remember that you can either choose to live your life looking for signs of failure, to reinforce where you see yourself in your own story, or find opportunities to take steps towards how you define success.

You know, if you don't want something to work out, you'll find a way for it not to work for you. So, if this is a lovely sign to stop doing something you don't want to work out, you do you.

But if you do want this to work out, you can and you will find another way to get on board. It might take some navigating, some late nights, some epic patience or even some extra cash, but you can accept your new reality, change it or leave.

The most important thing is that you don't get stuck in inertia. Make a choice, and make dang sure it aligns to your version of success, not someone else's.

You can be the role model you need to be for yourself this time. Ask yourself, 'Do I want this to be a STOP sign or a footnote in my story?' Make it a footnote in your story. (Then put it in your book!)

PART 4
YOU CAN DO IT!

YOU CAN DO IT!

In this final part of the book, remember to stay committed,
celebrate your achievements and start to enjoy the new life you
are leading. Know that if you are doing it right, you might need
to start the process all over again…

Chapter 12

STAYING STRONG

It's really, really, important to stay strong in your resolve (and boundaries!) as you share your news. As you do this, you'll be carefully balancing the need to make space to understand how others experience your evolution with being kind to yourself along the way. In this chapter, I outline strategies to communicate your needs as people respond in their own way, so you are prepared.

When you are in a committed relationship

You may choose to communicate your needs differently if you are in a committed relationship rather than if you are single.

When I was single, I didn't need to tell anyone if I wanted to quit my job or start a blog on the weekends. I didn't have any financial dependants or family commitments on the weekend.

So, shortly after I started dating my now spouse, I booked a holiday to New York. The thinking was that I was seeking inspiration and perhaps a change of scene would give me a boost in the right direction. I booked the flights online and simply flicked my spouse a calendar invitation for the dates I'd be overseas as an 'FYI'.

Well…

That night, my spouse came home and solemnly, calmly said, 'I noticed you booked a holiday to New York. The last time you went to New York, you, er… one: had a massive burnout; two: broke up with your partner; three: spent two weeks crying and shopping in SoHo; four: ruined your makeup at a Beyoncé concert; and five: renovated your life.

'So… is there something you want to tell me?'

Unbeknown to me, after receiving the invitation, my spouse had been methodologically losing their mind at work, worrying about what this really meant. I'd been spontaneous and didn't feel the need to involve them. I was using my own cash, I was my own boss, I could take holidays when I liked and all that (diva hair flick).

What I hadn't considered was the role of consultation in the decision. Prior to that moment, I'd spent the last decade as an independent woman. What I learned from my partner's feedback, which had been delivered with love, was that their concern wasn't about the trip itself but about me. Was I okay? Was I in my right mind? Had I lost the plot? Was this a red flag? If not, what did this mean?

While you mightn't have a plan to go to the other side of the world (or perhaps you might), the people who are important to you deserve to know in advance what your intentions are and what you are looking to do next.

This isn't about getting their approval, or feedback, or making it more comfortable for them; rather, this is about involving them in the process of your thinking. If someone is important to you, it can be a real kick in the gut for them if you make a major life decision without taking the time to let them know your rationale, your thinking, and that you've thought of them in relation to what that might mean.

By doing so, you are including them, showing them you trust them and that they play a significant enough role in your life to be consulted about major life decisions.

Some partners might feel excited about change. From experience, I can tell you that at some stage in your growth process – and this is pretty much a sure thing if you're making major changes around your career (remember, security is a biggie built into our DNA) – the majority of partners will freak out in some way.

This is really, really typical. Over time, it'll become clear whether they are on your team or can't accept your new reality. But for now, give them the benefit of the doubt.

As your partner gets their head around your new decisions, you might experience:

- underhanded comments undermining your process
- seeking credentials, or 'proof' that this works or will get you what you want
- being told that you've changed
- being asked if you are planning on leaving them.

All of these behaviours are your partner's way of seeking certainty. They are very typical, human responses.

Remember, as humans we 100 per cent crave certainty, and in partnerships this uncertainty is a biggie. We like to know where we stand. We like to feel safe and secure.

It is okay if your partner or intimate friends respond in this way in the short term as they get their heads around it. But it is not okay for that behaviour to become a part of the dynamic of your relationship long term.

Just be sure to keep a note of their initial 'getting their head around it' stage and, as you evolve, they will make a choice to dig their heels in to be unhelpful (resisting your change), or acknowledge their fear or uncertainty and give you space and trust to figure it out in a supportive, healthy way.

When someone gives you an ultimatum

Sadly, I do have experience of being given an ultimatum. It can be hurtful in the short term, however it's liberating and freeing in the long term.

When people give you an ultimatum, they are saying to you, 'I do not accept this change in your life,' and there may be nothing you can do to convince them otherwise.

This might give you the clarity you need to end a relationship that no longer serves you. If they can't get on board – BYE!

But before you cut them off, consider the possibility that there simply might be a miscommunication. If you are on the receiving end of an ultimatum, it can feel very hurtful. A helpful thing to remember is that everyone is managing their own boundaries, feelings and emotions. If someone cuts you off, it might be because they simply need time or space. It might be because they can't get their head around your choices. They may know you as 'someone else' and find it hard to see you as someone ever evolving.

In some instances, if you do receive an ultimatum, it might be because they have a very genuine concern for your safety or freedom. Sometimes the other person truly believes you are putting yourself in what they see as a potentially unsafe or risky situation, or something that seems to be completely out of the blue or at odds with the values they understand you to have.

I know plenty of people who have been in emotional, financial and physically unsafe, inequitable or unstable relationships where the power dynamic has been off. In these situations, those friends have been genuinely concerned about what they are seeing as red flags – for example, if they notice someone you are with is encouraging you to cut off ties with your friends, family or people you adore. As a result, they have not been shy about stepping in and saying 'I can't support your decision'.

If they have these concerns, they might pull out the last card in the deck: 'If you choose this, I can't do "us" anymore', or, 'This isn't you, I don't know this person anymore'.

Unfortunately, ultimatums in this instance deliver precisely what the person in control hopes for – social isolation. If you see this dynamic playing out with someone you care about, be sure to state your boundary around behaviour you do and don't accept, and let them know your door is always open.

An alternative to an ultimatum could be safe boundaries that practise acceptance for the person you care about. Example responses could include, 'I will always love and support you. I am always going to be here for you, but I can't support this choice,' or, 'I don't agree with what you have chosen, but I love you regardless and will always be here for you,' or, 'I need a break from this dynamic, but know it's because I can't get my head around this. I will always be your friend and I will always be here for you, regardless,' or even, 'I do need some space, but know you can call me in an emergency or if you are scared, and I will be there for you.'

These responses help the person in an unhelpful dynamic understand they have a network to reach out to when, and if, they make a decision to leave the relationship or remove themselves from the situation.

Back to you. If you are faced with an ultimatum, know that the person offering it is just trying to protect themselves. And time can be a real healer. You (both) might feel differently after some time to reflect. Be open to inserting a boundary and doing what you need to. Sometimes it just takes a little bit of trial and error until you land in the spot that feels right.

I have bumped into people years later who have given me an ultimatum in the past, and to my delight, there was a smile on their face, as there was on mine. Equally, I have been ignored in public by people who weren't ready to see me again, and I have definitely hidden in the loo from someone I wasn't ready to see just yet! So, it goes both ways.

Sometimes an ultimatum is also freedom after stepping away from something that isn't right for you. For example, I have heard back from people I have fired, or who had resigned, years later. While our circumstances took us in different directions – and I inserted a boundary by letting them go, or they did to find a workplace that was a better fit for them – I never stopped caring about them and hoping they were well. They were able to find a workplace that was the right fit for them, and I was freed up to find a team member who was the right fit for me.

When your partner is negative

This is incredibly common, particularly with couples that have been together for some time and have gone through a significant life change, such as deciding to have children, supporting a loved one through illness or grief, buying a house or relocating to a new area for one of their jobs.

All these changes both enrich your life and add subtle stressors which, if unaddressed (or if only discussed passive-aggressively in times of stress), can pop up when one member of the relationship starts to reflect on their life choices and seek changes. The idea that you and they have 'collectively suffered' and then you are opting out, or have identified another way before your partner has had a chance to process it, well, that's enough for them to struggle to focus on the positive when discussing a potential change.

The response of the person you love is more about their attachment to, and relationship with, the perception of risk, particularly financial risk. Remember this: when people rely on us, we become, in addition to wonderful, loving humans, a symbol of some form of security – whether that's through attention, love, food, finances or emotional support.

If you have children

In my experience of working with hundreds of coaching clients, the person who most commonly responds negatively to change is either the breadwinner, the recent breadwinner (when there's been a change in the dynamic of who brings home more money, and the status and power that can come with that) and/or the partner who more strongly associates their identity with financial security and social status.

It doesn't take a rocket scientist to figure out change seems to challenge the unspoken 'deal' that exists between partners, particularly those with children and where one person is contributing more financially while the other does the majority of the child-rearing. So often, the person who isn't the breadwinner plays a role that provides emotional support, attention, parenting, schooling, validation, meals and ferrying children around, and that can often, subconsciously, be seen as less valuable than bringing in the cash – you know, the 'real job'.

While it's rarely discussed explicitly, when it comes down to it in my sessions with clients, the real pain, hurt and confusion is caused by traditional gender roles around child-rearing.

One person pays the bills, the other pays in emotional support, but the bill-payer is perceived as more 'important'. This dynamic is outdated in Western culture, yes, but it is more prevalent than you might think in many modern-day relationships.

Irrespective of who is proposing the change, when children are involved, the start of a new journey for one member of the couple could be the dam-buster that has been years in the making. Don't forget that as you lean into new and exciting territory.

If your partner continues to be negative, reconsider whether this person is capable of supporting you in the way you deserve and need. Communicate your needs to ensure they are 100 per cent clear on what is required to continue to nurture this relationship. You might also arm yourself with examples of the impact of their negativity on your ability to take positive action, and how, ultimately, that will limit your ability to be a loving and supportive partner in their endeavours.

In my experience of supporting people whose partners are seeking change, I have found that a robust, emotionally honest conversation helps them understand that their fear is limiting the growth of the person they love. This causes them to reflect. From this place, they can then make a choice on whether they want to accept or reject the new reality.

One helpful way to give yourself courage to have the conversation is to think about it in terms of the type of relationship you would like to be in. Here are some examples:

- 'Do I want to be in an emotionally honest relationship or one where we pretend everything is fine?'
- 'Do I want to be scurrying around behind their back doing this work, or do I want this form of growth to be welcomed and seen as a good thing?'

- 'Am I okay with someone who's okay with me not being okay?'

This can be a compelling reframing when a spouse is responding negatively. You might be tempted to say, 'Don't worry about it!' or, 'It was just an idea!' or, 'Just joking!' I know that in the past I've certainly hidden in the toilet to stop myself from going back on an idea I've shared. (Sometimes you have to protect your future self from your self-sabotaging self!) But to have a healthy relationship built on honesty, you must stand your ground and find a way to get, if not entirely comfortable, used to feeling a little uncomfortable as you grow your confidence in sharing your needs.

Regardless of how your partner responds, it's also helpful to remember that their information (even if it's negative) is data to help you understand where they are at. If your growth is a shock to them, it's also a good chance to get on the same page. Even them being shocked is good data! 'How could they not know?' you might think. Aha! The mind-reader bias strikes again. You have to get used to sharing your needs with those you love and those who love and care about you.

If they are stunned you want to do something different, perhaps there's a way to include them in your thinking or bring their awareness to your point of view. If they do respond negatively, it's a big clue that they are uncomfortable. Getting curious can be a helpful step forward. Knowing where your partner stands, after a few conversations, can help you decide what is right for you. Just make sure that choice doesn't come at the cost of your happiness or your concern for their comfort. That's not an equitable balance of power – only one person wins there, and that person isn't you. (It's not the kids either, if you have them. In some way or another, as they grow they absorb and eventually mimic what they are exposed to. I know this all too well as I have supported thousands of people who replay family dynamics in the workplace. These are often referred to as patterns, as we outlined in Chapter 4.)

What to say and do when people freak out

As a result of all of the above, it is perfectly normal if people in your network freak out a little bit when you share with them that you are looking for personal growth. This will require patience on your end. If they stumble over their words, or don't respond as you would like, it can help to remember that this may be the first time they are hearing from you on this topic, or in this level of detail. Talking about an idea in theory and taking actions are two different things.

It may be coming completely from left field that you even had an intention of making a change in the first place. They might not agree with your decision or fully understand why you are making it, but you want to take the time to help them understand that you aren't doing this on a whim or for the high of trying something new.

To help them understand your decision and how it impacts them, and to help them respect it, here are some things that might help:

- Provide context by outlining your 'before' status. You would have done this in the first part of the Growth Cycle. By understanding how you are feeling, thinking and making decisions, they will be in a stronger position to get their head around why your changes are your logical next step in your growth.

- If relevant, outline how this will impact your relationship with them. How it impacts them is top-of-mind for them, remember.

- Offer to step them through the process you went through to get to your decision. Demonstrating your rigour will help those who care about you have faith you have thought through all the potential consequences. This might help them appreciate the level of logical thinking that has gone into your decision.

- They might ask, 'Why didn't you tell me you felt like this?' You might opt to share that until you did this process, you had an underlying feeling or inclination that some elements of your life were misaligned, but until going through this you weren't entirely clear on what they were; this process simply helped you see that you needed to make a few changes.

- Share with them what you need to succeed, and ask them for their help! Involving them in the process will help them see how important they are to you.

The other thing to remember is that all of the above is great practice for communicating your needs. It might feel odd, uncomfortable and potentially tiring at first, but over time it will become easier, and you will see the return of your energy and happiness.

Keep going. You've got this!

Unsubscribing from people-pleasing

If you're like me, you may feel happiest when others have their needs met. But who's looking after you? This is something that is really important to take into consideration as you start to make edits to your life.

Putting yourself in people-pleasing situations more often than you would like, or giving away your agency for someone else's comfort, is going to get in the way of you achieving great things. Let's look at some strategies to shift from people-pleasing to communicating your needs and feeling good about your choices and agency.

One way you can do that is by teaching yourself how to unsubscribe from a behaviour that puts someone else's happiness and comfort ahead of your own. To do that, you may need to go through a process of emotionally separating yourself from other people's versions of success by creating your own, letting go of other people's opinions of you through a process of fortifying and celebrating your unique take on success. The good news is that you have already gone through this process in Chapter 6. The next step is to start to make decisions that prioritise that, independent of external factors.

You are not responsible for other people's happiness

A nuance of people-pleasing is that it exacerbates the narrative that other people's happiness is contingent on your life choices.

If this rings true for you, creating ways to find more in your life may feel counterintuitive. You might wonder, 'How will I find more if I have to be X for my family/partner/ community?' (The X could represent anything. Examples might include strength, finances, support or presence.)

It can be helpful to remember that looking for more in your life doesn't mean you wish anyone else less. Rather, you're looking for ways to strengthen who you are so you can show up in life – really show up! And you're doing this so you can expand and grow and be your best self. A consequence of this is that you can be more for those you love – for your family, your friends, those you care about, those you serve and support and, of course, your community of choice.

If you are currently a support for your family, by aligning your life choices with who you're becoming you are able to be even more present, loving and creative. You can be a confident, loving, kind person who is living an authentic life and who can enable that in others purely through proximity.

If this causes you to feel uncomfortable, you might also be experiencing something just under the surface: either you have felt rejected or judged in the past for showing your true 'self', or you know the people in your life are in pain of their own, which causes them to want to keep you right by their side. And this is where guilt can start to set in and stop you from looking for more out of your life. Compassion can shift from genuine care into guilt and, eventually, resentment when you've prioritised someone else over your own happiness. (The concept of reflecting on your inner resentment is covered in greater detail in Chapter 8.)

If this is the case, it can be helpful to remember that your current reality doesn't affect your future reality, and there are productive ways to unsubscribe from prioritising other people's happiness above your own.

The first step is to stop analysing your life as a process of taking things away. Rather, you are going through this process to find more to life, and while that may mean some changes along the way, you are not stepping away. You are simply looking to stop thinking about your happiness as being contingent on someone else's. You are looking to create your own definition of success and autonomy to eventually share with others.

The second step is to create space that is uniquely yours, away from external influences and forces. No one can do personal enquiry as beautifully as you can, as no one knows you as well as you know yourself. At this step, many people opt out of looking for more – so if you are tempted to do this, know that you are not alone! The act of being by yourself and alone with your thoughts can feel daunting at times. Yet this is how we grow – through reflection and connecting our beliefs with our actions, through marrying our thoughts with our present. That's why reaching out for support – whether through a trained counsellor, a coach, or a trusted friend or family member – can be a helpful first step.

When I am tempted to stay small, or prioritise other people's requests or needs above my own, I personally find it helpful to remember that those I love sure don't love being around me when I'm feeling internally conflicted. They get my 'false self' then, when I'm physically present but mentally somewhere else. I have to work on checking in with myself and reminding myself to say no to events and expectations when I'm leaning towards people-pleasing to the extent that it takes me away from my core self. This helps me give myself some space to come back to myself and top up my energy tank. Through this process, I have discovered I am a deep introvert who gets personal strength, energy and clarity after time alone. Sometimes, during this alone time, I have a notepad and scribble down ideas. Other times I spend the day with only myself, and take myself out for lunch and dinner. Just bliss! Yet had I said yes without first checking in with myself, I may not have discovered this and would therefore be less aware of how to use it as a superpower.

For extroverted clients and friends of mine, they find going to a cafe, being around the buzz of other people for half an hour or an hour, is a great way to 'train' themselves into spending time alone without feeling isolated. Others like stepping through the exercises included in this book with a friend and gently sharing their ideas with someone they trust and respect. I typically ask them to do this with people who are naturally optimistic, or supportive of new ideas, as opposed to people who may at first be critical. It's a small thing, but it really helps grow your confidence muscle to expose your inner workings to people who are likely to be open to them at first glance.

The third step is to identify what you are craving more of in your dynamic with people you find yourself saying yes to. For example, perhaps you are wanting a more equitable balance of emotional labour. Maybe you crave to be seen in a new way. Perhaps you want to have the confidence to ask for more information from your boss before accepting a new assignment.

If what they are craving more of is not immediately coming to mind, some of my clients find it helpful to focus on what they are missing instead. You might reflect on what is currently missing from the relationships where you find yourself on people-pleaser autopilot mode. What makes this dynamic so, where you feel the need to appease as opposed to being seen as an autonomous equal? Examples might include, 'I am missing a two-way dialogue with my boss', or, 'I am missing having clarity on what I want to say yes to instead,' or, 'I'm missing feeling confident sharing my own point of view.'

Please note: it may be during this very enquiry, when you start thinking about the specifics, when your people-pleasing tendencies will go into overdrive. This is your default comfort zone saying, 'Hey! Let's stay in our comfort zone!' It is perfectly okay if this happens to you.

One realisation many of my clients have when interrogating these feelings is that they haven't experienced an equitable, autonomous, respectful, two-way relationship in some areas of their life. This can be a deeply profound and hurtful realisation. Others realise that when they do seek more in their life, they may lose someone they deeply care about. Certainly I've had that experience myself.

While it's true you might opt to step away from relationships, also know this: by communicating your needs, you also have the power to change a dynamic. I've seen this time and time again in my own life and in those of my clients. When communicating your needs, yes, some people might need a minute before they get used to them, but something else also can happen: they agree and get on board.

I remember having a conversation with one of my friends. She'd called for advice and I'd gone right into 'fix this problem' mode. After the call, I felt strange, but I couldn't quite put my finger on why. I thought she wanted a solution, so I got right onto that, just like I would at work! So, why didn't it sit right with me? Through reflection, I realised I'd gone into people-pleasing work mode – my comfort zone. I thought to myself, 'Would I have wanted a solution or a friend at that moment?'

When we next spoke, I apologised. I told her that after reflecting, I realised I'd gone into 'fix it' mode, and I wondered whether she might have just appreciated a listening ear all those weeks ago! That admission, from a place of 'I think I can be better than this, so bear with me as I figure out how to be better than this,' opened a really beautiful, completely new level of depth between us. Her openness and grace enabled us to start an open conversation about each other's needs – where they were similar and where they were different – from a place of genuine care, judgement-free. As a result, we ended up chatting about what our friendship could be like. It was the loveliest negotiation I've ever had! Without that reflection, the dynamic would have continued – or, simply put, she would have stopped calling and I would have been none the wiser.

So often, the fear of other people's reactions stops us from taking action. This is not people-pleasing. This is fear. And if we want to move away from this dynamic, we must take safe steps of action. The good news is that there are always safe steps we can take. They don't all need to be big conversations. Sometimes we can simply make small edits to the way we choose to communicate or create space for ourselves before we default to saying 'yes' – or, in my case, 'fixing'!

When this does come up, know this: you don't actually need to take action until you are sure it's the right step and safe for you to do so. The people you support, love and serve will require consultation along the way, which I outline in further detail earlier in this chapter. But know there are so many steps you can take before you even involve those you care about in your story! These are all things you can do discreetly and safely.

You are not letting others down by reflecting on your needs. Rather, you are better able to support them by becoming more of who you already are. In some instances, you will also be saving yourself.

To get, sometimes you have to let go

Here's something that sounds easy but could take time to get your head around: surrendering to what others will think, whether you hear about it or not, will set you free. It will also help you create the space to focus on doing the work you need to do to grow. The act of mentally releasing others' thoughts and judgements on how you show up in the world will create space in your mind to focus on what you want and need.

Sounds easy, right? Wrong! Well, at least for me and many of the people I've coached. It takes time to unsubscribe from defaults and subscribe to actions that actually serve us.

I'll give you a work-related example. My early career was in public relations. My job was to make someone as well-known as possible. This meant getting clients interviewed on TV and radio, and featured on magazine covers. The clients who became the most well-known were those who had a succinct message, were relevant in the moment and who, after releasing a piece of work, let go of controlling how others would respond to it and didn't block others from understanding, interpreting, analysing, reviewing and judging it.

Firstly, they surrendered control by handing me the reins to create a narrative around their work. They then released control by letting go of shaping the message, to enable the media to create their unique perspective.

While these people were all very talented and committed, they didn't become well-known solely because of the quality of their work. They became well-known because they let go. They got comfortable with the idea of others having a point of view about them, whether it was positive or negative, dissenting or agreeing.

While you might not have aspirations of becoming well-known (or you might!), I find this a helpful example to reflect on. These people chose to surrender control of what others thought and instead focused on what they could control: the choices they made, the quality of their work and communicating it in their own way. They chose to own their inputs and outputs, not how others would interact with them.

Applying this to a personal situation, it can be helpful to imagine a world where the first voice you hear is yours – your internal voice, guiding you. You have done the hard work in creating space for yourself and creating your own version of success. To enjoy that success, sometimes you have to let go, and practise tuning into your own voice and letting that reverberate in the world.

The cost of people-pleasing

What is the cost of not having your work or perspective heard, to you and to those you love?

I am confident that millions of people who have valuable, rich and new insights to share with the world simply don't. One example I have discovered in almost every instance of supporting clients who come from a research, health or academic background is that putting themselves out there, communicating their view or findings, and being heard and successful – especially if they aren't the world-leading expert in their field (although in some cases they actually are!) – is an exceptionally difficult concept for them to wrap their head around.

Why? Because there's always someone who knows more than you, right? And when your background is one of academic rigour, how can you possibly get comfortable with the idea of saying 'here's my point of view' without thinking, 'But there is so much more to learn about my topic of speciality! I simply can't know it all!'

While it's true we can't know it all, I'd like to suggest that we stop pretending there'll be a time when we do! We'll never know it all. Even if we did, I'm certain the world would change around us, forcing us to adapt once again.

Instead, I suggest we stop worrying about what we don't know and start sharing what we do know. It is powerful and liberating to say, 'This is what I know for sure, and this is what I'm now curious about as a result.' It sets you free from expectation and raises your confidence when you shift to owning what you know and stepping into curiosity, and moving away from judgement.

I recently heard the CEO of Hello Seven, Rachel Rodgers, conduct an interview with a guest on her podcast who said that she never felt impostor syndrome because she committed to owning her lane. I love that idea. By doubling down on what you do know for sure, you lower anxiety around others' interpretations and pave the way to share your own point of view from a place of generosity and strength.

What I am outlining here is a powerful mindset shift and an opportunity to reflect. How often do you worry about what you don't know? What if you started to confirm what you are certain about and, as Oprah might say, what you know for sure?

What you focus on gets your attention. What gets your attention gets your time. What gets your time designs your life.

It is possible to reframe fear into excitement (and if that's a stretch, try being curious first). You can do that by ensuring you give yourself the best possible chance to succeed by focusing your attention on the benefits of showing up as yourself. By choosing to focus on ways to let go of needing to appease others and instead directing attention towards living an authentic life in congruence with how you define success, you are already well on your way to directing energy towards a life that, indeed, has more – one that looks like success to you.

When you find this challenging, you can simply start paying attention to what you focus your attention on or find yourself reacting to. Focusing on others who mightn't have plans to ever accept and support your future steps holds you back from investing time into you. By investing time to map out what having more in your life could look like, you are owning the narrative. You are in charge of the choices you make.

Reframing conflict as assertiveness

A fear of conflict has limited so many of my clients from communicating assertively in the past. Why?

More often than not, it's the way they've been raised or influenced by their culture. Being told to only speak when they've been spoken to, or to acquiesce to someone else's preferences, or simply being on the receiving end of aggression from other people's discomfort, is enough to make any rational person think twice before communicating! If you don't feel safe sharing your opinion, how can you get into the habit of asking for what you need?

I see this manifested a huge amount in the workplace as fear of feedback. I estimate the majority of employees actively avoid feedback that could enable their career goals purely out of fear of 'conflict'.

This avoidance becomes a self-reinforcing cycle, which many of my clients aren't even fully aware of before undergoing reflection exercises around addressing and meeting their needs. The by-product is that they are constantly uncomfortable, uncertain and, at times, double-guessing their position. As we discussed in Chapter 1, when you are in your comfort zone, feeling like this can become 'normal', and it can be easy to forget that there is another way.

It is a slow process unsubscribing from people-pleasing, and it starts by reframing a fear of conflict into a way to have your needs met using healthy, assertive communication skills. When your communication is in alignment with having your needs met or enabling a future goal, you will be more likely to feel confident about approaching a conversation from a place of assertiveness. You can't ever control how someone else reacts, but you can control how you prepare for a conversation, being clear about your intent and what you need.

Where to start? Training yourself to communicate effectively is something that is completely within your control, and it starts with your internal dialogue. Only you can control how you communicate. Whether you like it or not, if you are unable to communicate rationally or helpfully, you won't have your needs met.

By focusing on ourselves, and checking in with ourselves, we are so much more likely to respond to disagreements in perspectives differently and diffuse them, and (here's the gem) see conflict entirely differently as well.

I have had hundreds of people say to me that they no longer see feedback as conflict as a result of undergoing Happiness Concierge training. Instead, they see it as valuable data to drive their performance forward. The reason they feel this way is that they've been supported to communicate their needs in helpful ways.

The first question for you to reflect on is, 'How can I have my needs met every day?' I'm not talking about your dream meal or wardrobe (although that could be part of it!); rather, I'm suggesting you ask yourself, 'What does it take for me to show up as my best self? What needs to go into the tank so that I can show up as my most compassionate, kind, thoughtful, clever and awesome self?'

In an interview with Oprah, Iyanla Vanzant speaks about the idea of filling our cups beautifully. She says, 'My cup runneth over. What comes out of the cup is for y'all. What's in the cup is mine.'

There are so many elements, some big and some small, that help us to show up as our best self. In the 1940s, psychologist Abraham Maslow proposed that to reach self-actualisation, the following needs had to be met first: physiological needs (such as food and clothing), safety and security (such as a steady job and a roof over our heads), love and belonging (such as respectful relationships and friendships) and esteem (such as prestige or a feeling of accomplishment). This is called Maslow's Hierarchy of Needs. I have found it such a helpful reference when supporting clients and reflecting on how I show up in the world.

There is evidence to suggest Maslow's celebration of self-actualisation was inspired by his experiences with the Blackfoot First Nations people. In this context, the health of a community is endorsed as a communal focus, and self-actualisation is seen as an innate superpower each person is born with. It is the job of a community to create the space and support for each individual to realise it. Teju Ravilochan writes:

> 'While Maslow saw self-actualization as something to earn, the Blackfoot see it as innate. Relating to people as inherently wise involves trusting them and granting them space to express who they are ... rather than making them the best they can be. For many First Nations, therefore, self-actualization is not achieved; it is drawn out of an inherently sacred being who is imbued with a spark of divinity.'

I find the concept of everyone being inherently sacred beautiful. The context of each person positively impacting their wider community, family or group of people in their care is a wonderful reference for people leaders. Using this as a guiding principle and lens for decision-making and action during times of change or stress – such as a pandemic, or a change in someone's personal circumstances – can help steer responsible decisions affecting an employee's 'full self'.

With this guidance, they are able to shift from an output focus to an input focus by asking themselves, for example, 'What does my team need in order to show up, and what can I do to support this?'

I'll give you a small, tangible example. I would often find myself internally eye-rolling in meetings some days. Dang, I was always mad about something in my head, but when I interrogated it… nope, I had no answer. There was no one tangible to blame, until I realised (and please feel free to laugh openly) that whenever I felt mad, it meant I'd forgotten to eat that day. I'd worked through so many lunch breaks in my past it had never occurred to me that I could be the person responsible for my grumpiness! Grr.

My mum told me that growing up I was this happy wee child, but watch out world if anyone talked to me before breakfast. Rawr! She tells this story of a grumpy little rage bucket who'd have a banana put in front of her until she mentally defrosted. It made me laugh because bananas are now my favourite food. Perhaps it's the potassium – who knows?

What that meant in the workplace was that, if I hadn't eaten, I'd be very direct and to the point, and lack any capacity to actively listen. Can you see how something that was my responsibility started to have a flow-on effect on everyone around me? Such a small thing as asking myself, 'What do I need to do to show up as my best self today?' caused me to realise that something in my control, such as setting a timer for lunch (true story), could have a pretty epic effect. All of a sudden, I had mental energy for problem-solving, listening and being generally charming to be around.

Back to you. What to do with this information? Here is an exercise I step through with my clients to support them to ask, 'Are my needs being met? What needs have to be met so I can show up in the world as I intend?'

Self-reflection

Step One: What needs do I need to have met every day?

_____

_____

_____

_____

Examples:
- *Food, water, coffee, shower, clean clothes*
- *Exercise, walks, time alone*
- *Time to talk, time to reflect, time to laugh, time to read*
- *To be heard, valued, seen, understood and recognised*
- *Time with a special person, to decompress and download.*

Which of these are my responsibilities?

_____

_____

_____

Which of these are other people's responsibilities, or things I expect from others?

_____

_____

_____

What is within my control? What expectations are reasonable?

_____

_____

_____

How can I communicate my needs? What are the outlets?

_____

_____

_____

How can I communicate my needs as my best self?

_____

_____

_____

You now have the fundamentals clear on what you need so you can show up as your best self. Provided you're comfortable to proceed – and it's okay if you'd like to take time to pause – the next step is to look in further detail at how you can feel heard and understood more often.

If you regularly experience assertive communication, direction or feedback as conflict, you may have had an experience in the past where you didn't feel heard, recognised, valued or seen. That's the thing about experiences – they shape you and stay with you until you can make sense of them! They pretty much pack some snacks, jump in your mental backpack and come along to every experience that looks or sounds like one you've had before. That's why it's so valuable to unpack these sorts of experiences with someone you trust or a great professional therapist, coach or counsellor.

I'd like to invite you to perform a gentle enquiry, to outline places where you do feel heard and understood. As you do this, you might like to also extend to where you don't feel seen and heard.

Self-reflection

Step Two: How can I feel heard and understood more often?

_____

_____

_____

_____

Thought starters:

- *When do I most feel heard at work, and outside of work?*
- *When do I feel seen and valued by my partner, and/or special people around me?*
- *When do I most feel understood by those around me?*

Focusing on when we most feel seen, heard, valued and recognised helps reinforce what's working well. Chances are, when we experience these things, we communicate with confidence and without abandon. We don't double-guess ourselves; instead, we speak our minds and feel safe doing so!

Conversely, through doing this exercise, circumstances might become clear where you don't have those experiences. It is typically in these circumstances where miscommunication can occur, leading us into 'fight, flight or freeze' territory – the 'panic zone' we discussed in Chapter 1. In this zone, adrenaline is firmly in the driver's seat, and we are unlikely to communicate in helpful ways. Consequently, we are less able to hear information from a place of curiosity and understanding. Instead, we might interpret assertiveness as conflict, clarity as critique, and so on. If this is relevant to your experience, this is a neat opportunity for you to pause and ask, 'How could I get more of my needs met in this instance so I can have great conversations, communicate confidently and feel understood?' You are questioning your surroundings from a place of abundance ('there has to be more') instead of scarcity ('there has to be less').

Here's a fun exercise that builds upon the previous one. What could a world look like where your needs are met, in a life that has more? I often share these thought-starters with my clients.

With this information, you have an opportunity to start reviewing opportunities to communicate your needs, reduce fear of how others will respond and focus on you.

Self-reflection

Step Three: If my needs were met, what would that look like?

I would feel heard and valued at/in _____

_____

_____

_____

I would take ownership of my needs by _____

_____

_____

I would stop taking ownership of others' needs by _____

_____

_____

_____

I would speak up when _____

_____

_____

_____

As a result, I would feel/could experience/could focus on

_____

_____

_____

Small steps add up to huge wins

When we work with clients at Happiness Concierge to help them communicate with confidence in the workplace, we focus on creating opportunities for them to experience small wins by asking for what they need. Small wins, as we've discussed in earlier chapters, help us practise a new skill in small ways as we build our confidence. By focusing on what they can control (how they respond and communicate), clients often find amazing opportunities to try small ways to have their needs met to lower their fear of conflict and help them experience moments of productive assertiveness.

One tool we use to great effect in the workplace is the Sourcing Feedback Challenge. Many of our clients triple their return on investment in the services of Happiness Concierge solely from this exercise. It's so effective because it puts the employee in the driver's seat of their career progression, and it grows confidence as well as skill. Here's how it works:

- Source one piece of feedback to drive your performance forward from someone you respect. This might be a leader or a colleague. It should be someone outside your immediate friend group, as friends will tend to lovingly tell you what you want to hear instead of something that can take you to your next step professionally.

- Frame it in a positive way. At Happiness Concierge, we say to only give feedback if it helps someone take a positive step forward or develop in their career, or if it validates a great behaviour. By asking for one piece of feedback framed from the perspective of 'one thing for me to focus on to drive my performance forward', it encourages the person you are asking to laser in on one tangible piece of feedback (as opposed to a passionate word salad) that will help you ace work.

- Once you've sourced this piece of feedback, your challenge is to ask questions until you understand it. Yep, many employees tell us they have no idea what the feedback they receive actually means, and they are unsure how to address it or bring it back up with their manager. This step helps you practise taking ownership of something you need to understand and action on a very practical level.

- Action that piece of feedback, or take a step towards actioning that feedback.

- Circle back to the person who gave you the feedback and give them a status update to let them know how you're taking action.

This is an extremely powerful exercise, and I urge you to consider giving it a go. If it sounds too easy, answer this: when was the last time you asked for specific feedback from your manager outside of a performance review? If you have never done this, why not? If you have done this, did you action the feedback you received? What were the results? Does your manager know? If not, is there an opportunity to circle back to them on this?

Most of the time, when I pose the above to a learning group, the majority of people admit they haven't sourced feedback since their past performance review. Often, in our passion for learning, we can forget to action the feedback and reflect on the results. The action and reflection is where growth lives.

Start in your inner circle

A tool I personally use when I'm looking to gain confidence with assertive communication is to ask myself what I need and want in any given interaction, and how I can let the person involved know (if it's appropriate to do so). I find that the smallest opportunities are the best ways to practise assertive communication. Here are a few examples:

- I'm a wreck when I'm hungry, and I also don't enjoy cooking. As a people-pleaser and perfectionist, I do get myself into a tangle doing things that certainly don't bring me joy. It's quite the conundrum. Instead of letting resentment grow around dinnertime, I have started asking, 'Who's going to make dinner tonight?' and then pausing before I go into people-pleasing action mode and offer to make it myself. Nine times out of ten, my partner, who loves to cook and is great at it, offers to cook. That then allows me to say, 'Great, I'll leave it to you and I'll do the dishes?' They get to chill after making an awesome meal; I can enjoy my evening and listen to a podcast while I load the dishwasher later on. Assertive communication, no conflict.

- When I get the wrong coffee order, I now take it back. I simply let them know what my order was and that another order seems to have made its way to me. This sounds so minor, but it's taken me time to speak up about this and then be quiet once I've been assertive! As I do it more often, I am becoming less abrasive, kinder in my delivery and more comfortable internally with asking for my needs to be met, too.

- When I'm in team meetings, I now make asking for feedback on my leadership part of every meeting. As a result, I am creating space for my team members to practise giving feedback so they grow, and I am hearing valuable insights into growing the business, training my ego out of existence, and being present and aware of what my team needs in order to succeed. It means assertive communication from my team and a fair amount of discomfort for me internally, but it's what I signed up for – I want to learn how to walk the talk so I can lean into that feeling with less conflict and more curiosity.

By unsubscribing to people-pleasing, you are also no longer working for free. You are resigning from a job you don't get paid to do and that no longer serves you; a job that keeps you small and further away from your fullest self – the job of appeasing others.

***

We've spoken about a number of strategies for how to clarify your needs and have them met, and to avoid fear of conflict preventing you from communicating your needs. Practise asking for what you need and you will discover something really lovely emerging: you communicate with more kindness, grace and, eventually, influence. Over time, you'll also see conflict as an opportunity to reach a shared understanding, as opposed to it simply being two sides in dispute.

Chapter 13

ASKING FOR MORE

As you level up your expectations, standards and boundaries, your world will start to look very different.

You will look at relationships differently. You will see your work from a different perspective. You may see things you hadn't noticed before. And in this space is the opportunity for you to achieve absolutely anything you desire. When you expect more, you don't settle for anything less in the pursuit of achieving your goals.

Here are some techniques many of my clients rave about when it comes to asking for more as their standards for success evolve.

Tell people what you want more of

As you clarify what it is you want more of, the next step is to… tell the world about it! When people know what you want more of, they can keep you in mind if they hear of anything aligned with what you're moving towards.

I encourage my clients to talk less about what doesn't inspire them and talk more about what they want to do more of in future. You don't need to update your LinkedIn, for example, or tell your manager you're thinking of doing more in a different direction. What you can do is simply share what it is you are looking to do more of with your network (be it your colleagues, friends or family), and let them know it's okay to keep you in mind if they come across anything in that area.

For example, let's say you are a project manager who has identified, through this process, that you are wanting to move towards pursuing your love of writing. You might share with your colleagues or friends, 'I have realised recently that I really enjoy writing and I'd love to dedicate more time to that. If you hear of any opportunities to do copywriting, or creative writing, let me know. If, for example, there are any projects at work that need a writing element, if I can fit it around my existing job, do think of me.'

See how simple that is? People can't help you to find more of what you are interested in without you telling them about it. Another benefit is that you don't need to have every part of your next step mapped out in order to ask for more. You can figure it out as you go.

It's important to frame this request for more in the positive. This is why sharing what you're looking for, or doing more of, is so powerful. People who care about you want to support your genuine desire. So, when it comes from a place of lacking (for example, 'I hate my job! Find me a job I don't hate!'), it's harder for them to authentically 'pitch you', or back you from a selling point of negativity. Conversely, when they know you are seeking more from a place of energy, enthusiasm and genuine interest, it opens a world of possibilities.

The people we know effectively become our 'cheerleaders', letting others know if and when they hear of anything aligned with our 'more of' requests. Keep it positive, and use it as a great chance to rehearse what you are looking for more of. Over time, it will become easy, and as you grow, so will your curiosities and requests and, consequently, the opportunities that land on your desk.

People you want to know are just one introduction away

Did you know that weak-tie networks, the people who are 'one contact removed' from people you know really well, are more likely to have access to valuable opportunities relevant to your career that you mightn't know about? This is why telling others what you want more of is so powerful. To develop your weak-tie network, focus on what you might have in common with someone you admire or respect but whom you've never met (yet). This is where a guided introduction from someone you trust and respect can work wonderfully. This works so well when you approach it from a place of learning. A fun rule I like to use for my own networking is, 'Who is three steps ahead of me that I could learn from?'

For example, as you reflect on what you want more of, you might identify an interest in surrounding yourself with entrepreneurs who are making a living out of what they love. As you share with your immediate network (your strong ties) what you are wanting more of, you can easily add this on: 'Is there anyone in your network who is running their own business and would be open to a connection? I'd love to ask them a few questions on how they started their business to grow my understanding in this area.'

Nurture your network

In a 75-year longitudinal study of the physical and emotional wellbeing of poor and affluent males, it was discovered that one factor was the best predictor of happiness: the quality of close relationships. Diversifying our 'joy portfolio' through quality relationships is a more apt predictor of happiness, essentially. These, coupled with stretch goals to keep learning, pave the way for a meaningful life on your own terms.

As you expect more from yourself and those in your life, you also have the opportunity to develop incredible friendships and relationships that not only support your goals but literally increase the quality of your health and wellbeing.

Be sure to reflect on not only the scope of your network but the quality of it, too. I have discovered in my own steps towards looking for more in my life, the simple act of asking different questions, sharing different thoughts and wanting more from my friendships and relationships has enabled me to ask hard questions that I feel I would not have had the courage or confidence to ask in my younger years!

Remember that friend I mentioned in the previous chapter who called with a problem, and I went into 'fix it' mode only to realise later that was not what she needed? That situation got me thinking: what if we could lovingly negotiate our relationships as we ask for and expect more from ourselves and those we invite into our world? And how can we take ownership of expecting more in our relationships?

Always evolving, your relationships are a direct reflection of the energy you contribute to them. When you shift your awareness, you have the opportunity to ask for, and share, more in different ways. My friend was graceful enough to share that she'd been reflecting on that conversation, too. Without that admission, might we ever have asked for, and expected, more from each other? Maybe; maybe not.

The point is that your existing relationships can get one heck of an upgrade when you pay them the attention you want more of. Always leading with what you can contribute differently paves the way to getting relationships that reflect what you want more of (or maybe less of, in my experience!).

Chapter 14

CELEBRATE THE WINS

Research has revealed that in the endless pursuit of motivating employees, there exists one foundational principle that keeps people engaged and creatively fulfilled: the pursuit of achievement and continual improvement towards goals. This has been referred to as the 'progress principle', which we discussed in Chapter 11.

The same applies for making any change. When you feel you are making progress towards your goals, your efficacy develops, your confidence grows, and your beliefs are reinforced and fortified.

If you are like me, you will push on ahead without pausing for a moment to congratulate yourself! I used to think that celebrating was like taking the foot off the pedal. What I have learned though, with support, is that celebrating wins helps you effectively create space between yourself and that thing you've been doing. Through space, you can see your achievement for what it is – very awesome and impressive – and taking that moment to let it sink in allows you to reflect on how far you have come.

It is hugely important, and I can't rave about it enough. Since stopping to celebrate the small wins, I have found myself happier, calmer and more readily able to speak about my accomplishments without playing them down for what I once thought was other people's comfort. I'm proud of my accomplishments. They don't define who I am, but you know what? I'm proud of who I've become. My goal is that you too will be able to create opportunities to remind yourself of this fact – and believe it.

Self-reflection

Set yourself up for celebrating success by taking a moment to outline:

What could a small win look like?

_____

_____

_____

What will I do to celebrate?

_____

_____

_____

Who could I celebrate with?

_____

_____

Can I give myself permission to pat myself on the back even if I have a tough week or a setback?

_____

_____

Nutting out the answers to these types of questions can be helpful in giving yourself grace and support as you navigate your next steps. Remember, you have the Achievement Audit tool included in Chapter 2 to refer to whenever you would like to top up your accomplishment tank!

Deflating moments don't have to derail you

As you start to make changes, you'll hit bumps in the road – whether it's your network not getting as excited as you are about your change, or something not going to plan.

I understand how deflating it can feel when something doesn't go to plan or, to be quite frank, it feels too hard. It can be really de-energising. It will be tempting to blame yourself in those moments for why you haven't taken action or haven't held the agreement you've made with yourself – big time! But they are simply bumps in the road on the route you're on, and by focusing on them you are giving your power away.

These things aren't happening *to* you. They are happening *for* you. The only thing you can control is what you choose to do as a result of the circumstances around you.

These moments can be deflating, but don't let them be derailing.

To give you an example of some deflating moments, here are some examples of negative feedback I got from real-life customers who attended some of my early classes:

- 'The bird in the red dress was a bit much.'
- 'Rachel, look, I didn't like you at first. Too… smiley.'
- 'This stuff's a bit cliche.'
- 'I'd love to work for you, is it okay if I solicit my own clients through your business for my own?'

And my personal favourite:

- 'No.'

That's all someone wrote on one feedback form: 'No'. Technically, I'd categorise that as 0/10.

I've got it saved in my cupboard somewhere to remind myself that there will always be someone who needs to express negativity, and that has nothing to do with me. Being able to share those moments, and get validation from people I love and who can help me see the 'funny' in them, has helped me shift shock into a great reminder that sometimes it's really not about me. To paraphrase artist Dita Von Teese, you can be the ripest, juiciest peach and there will always be someone who hates peaches.

With the gift of hindsight, the benefit of experience and the support of those who know me and love me, I am reminded that for every deflating moment, there are thousands of positives and millions of moments where I've made a positive impact – where the simple act of being myself, being open about who I am and 'owning it' has made me a role model to thousands of people. If Rachel Service can do it, they can do it, too! Now, if I had let those deflating moments define me or cause me to stop doing what I love, or if I had paused to give them any more airtime than they warranted, you wouldn't be reading this book right now. Boo!

My business wouldn't exist. I wouldn't have impacted millions of people across the globe with this work. And that would have given the people who wrote those negative critiques, people who won't ever find this work their flavour, more power to make me smaller. No. Not on my watch. That was not the agreement that I made with myself. The agreement

I made was this: 'If just one person in each workshop finds these tools helpful, that is success.'

Thousands of people later, I know these tools work for the people who want them to.

Choosing to share your process

It's easy to entertain the thought that you're the only one capable of changing, especially when people in your immediate network aren't displaying the things, activities and ideas you want more of.

For this reason, you might have some trepidation towards sharing your process with people you care about.

But there's something really cool that happens once you start getting curious and dipping your toe in the scary or 'but I've never talked about this with my friends' conversation pool. Experience tells me that our most humbling experiences can actually serve as the biggest contributors to positive change – if we're willing to change the narrative around what they mean to us after going through acknowledgement, healing and sometimes grief.

Sparking action is usually an emotional response to your own internal 'breaking point', when you realise that feeling in control is a priority. And sharing this experience can be a huge 'aha' moment for those who love you to truly understand what you have been experiencing and why you are seeking change.

The same is true for new conversations with people you know. Here are some guiding principles that can give you the confidence to have a conversation with people you care about:

- Be specific about what you are talking about. Specificity is respectful communication in action. If you have made your decision, don't pretend you are still making up your mind. Be forthright and give the person you're talking to the most time you can to absorb the new (to them) reality.

· Be as clear as you can when you know what you want to do next. If you are uncertain, be open to thinking out loud about what a next step might be.

· There is no prize for growth you can get from anyone but yourself. Instead of seeking applause, focus on your own validation as a recognition that you are on the right path.

If you do choose to share your process with others, invite them into your story. Resist the temptation to say they should do it too; no one can grow unless they decide to and want to. While everyone's growth process is unquestionably unique, believe it or not, despite doing all this work, you are not 'ahead' of anyone else. Your friends, family and colleagues are not incapable of growing along with you, you know. In fact, this is one of the promises my spouse and I made to each other on getting married. We made a commitment to continually grow and celebrate the pursuit of living a life that suits each one of us individually. The work from here is not in rushing someone else to their next step but in supporting their progress, in their own time, in their own way – just as we need to do for ourselves.

Expect to start again if you're doing it right

'Shoshin: Beginner's mind.'
– Zen Buddhist mindset

After implementing your action steps, as you become more comfortable, you will move from your learning zone to your comfort zone. Congrats!

As you move into your comfort zone... guess what? Some of you will outgrow some of your choices all over again.

If I haven't been explicit about this in the book prior to now, I want to make it clear that if you are growing, you are changing. And if you are changing, chances are, you'll outgrow your new choices. This is a great thing. In fact, you should be proud of this!

If you do find yourself outgrowing the choices you have made in this cycle, invite yourself to come back to the tools I've given you in this book to ask yourself the same questions six months, one year and several years from now. In what ways have you changed and evolved? What could stay, and what areas of your life could do with a review?

Regularly looking at your life from a place of greater perspective helps you make choices that reflect who you have become. Iterate as you go and have fun!

The great thing about growth is that it's a cyclical process. Continuous development and learning keeps our ego at bay and prevents us from becoming complacent.

The Growth Cycle you have learned about in this book has been designed to enable you to continue to grow, and to pass those lessons on to the important people you love and care for.

So, if and when you find yourself having those itchy feelings again of 'there has to be more', you can pull out your well-loved copy of this book and start at step one: pairing self-reflection with self-discipline to relearn who you've become and who you'll go on to become.

By then, you'll have new needs. You'll have different wants. You'll have different expectations.

You'll want different things, because you know what? You'll be different. As a result of taking the steps in this book, you will have changed. You will see things differently.

Challenging yourself to be true to yourself is an endless process. With this guide, my intention is for you to have the tools to continue to rediscover yourself and own what makes you unique and brilliant – what makes you feel most like yourself.

AFTERWORD

Why do we want more?

I believe the reason we run into problems as grown-ups is because we don't know where to start. No one sits us down at a certain age and says, 'Now… here is how you get everything you want in life!' (Wouldn't that be nice!)

When we do find out what it takes, it can come as quite a shock to realise the ownership we need to take to get more out of life. So, at some point, we need to make the decision to take ownership and make some decisions for ourselves.

When you have a problem, you also have the power to create a solution.

One thing I have noticed that is rarely discussed in the pursuit of getting more out of life is the idea of compromise. It is absolutely possible, with choices and support and resources, to have everything you want in life. As long as you're willing to say no to some things. As long as you're willing to make some hard choices. You have to make an effort, after all.

I think compromise has a bad reputation. I believe compromise is a good thing. What we're willing to compromise on and what we're not reveals our values, our deal breakers, the way we do business and who we are. It reveals our priorities.

If you don't want to do the work to compromise, you cannot expect a different outcome to the one you're experiencing right

THERE HAS TO BE MORE

now. I have learned that you cannot grow and outsource the compromising, the heavy lifting, the hard work.

It takes time to unsubscribe from expectations and assumptions about what your life is 'supposed' to look like. In some cases, it can take rewiring how you think entirely.

But when you get clear on what you want, and you develop the belief that you can do it (or at least figure it out) and that you believe you deserve to feel fulfilled, an amazing thing starts to happen: you start showing up for yourself. You start listening to your needs. You start making the decisions that control your life. You become the protagonist. You start to see there is so much more out there for you!

You'll see the results of putting effort into what you want. You will stop expecting a return for making the minimum effort in life.

If you live a life of service to others in any capacity, growth is a necessary part of the job description. Holding yourself to your standard of success might look different to what those who love and support you expect, but it will mean you never have to rely on someone else to define your future.

When it hasn't been about you for a long time, it can be really hard to see yourself as the person you're interested in becoming. To find out what you're capable of, to remember who you are, sometimes you have to take.

What if, instead of thinking about what there is to lose, you focused on what you could gain? What if, instead of putting other people's expectations first, you created your own? What if, instead of letting fear take the steering wheel, you took one small step towards what suits you best?

What all change starts with is an unwavering conviction in the belief that there is more to life. Instead of worrying what could go wrong, you need to think: what is the true cost of not taking action?

You have your own permission slip inside of you. You can give yourself permission.

You don't need the world to catch up to you to start your side project. You don't need to wait for others to 'get it' to put your hand up for that job. You don't need to wait for your boss to fire you from a job you hate to resign.

It's okay if you feel lonely at times, if you experience push-back. In fact, plan for it! It's okay if you want to rethink some of your choices and press 'undo' after being assertive with what you want.

But you must persist. Push through the short-term pain to gain your freedom. I promise you it is worth it.

Do it for you. Do it for those who love you, those who care about you.

Do it for those you'd love to show one day.

When I was in my twenties, I lived with my grandmother. As I got ready to go out one evening and asked her, 'How do I look?' she grabbed me by the wrist, pulled me towards her and said, 'Don't waste a minute. Don't waste a moment.'

If I could talk to my gran now, I'd tell her, 'I did it. I got burnt out – a few times – but I never gave up. I never gave up on myself. It took me some time to figure out how to be a grown-up my way, but I did it. I spent lots of time figuring it out, but I didn't waste a moment.'

Over to you. You've got this.

Next steps and resources

Sign up at rachelservice.com for the *There's Got To Be More* resources and do the exercises with a friend!

REFERENCES AND FURTHER READING

AC Shilton, 'You Accomplished Something Great. So Now What?', *The New York Times*, 28 May 2019, <nytimes.com/2019/05/28/smarter-living/you-accomplished-something-great-so-now-what.html>.

AH Maslow, 'A theory of human motivation', *Psychological Review*, vol. 50, no. 4, 1943, pp. 370–396.

Alison Wood Brooks, 'Get Excited: Reappraising Pre-Performance Anxiety as Excitement', *Journal of Experimental Psychology*, vol. 143, no. 3, 2014, pp. 1144–1158.

Andrew P Hill & Thomas Curran, 'Multidimensional Perfectionism and Burnout: A Meta-Analysis', *Personality and Social Psychology Review*, vol. 20, no. 3, 2016, pp. 269–288.

Carl Singleton, J James Reade & Alasdair Brown, 'Going With Your Gut: The (In)accuracy of Forecast Revisions in a Football Score Prediction Game'. *SSRN Electronic Journal*, 2018.

Cinthia Benitez, Kristen P Howard & Jennifer S Cheavens, 'The effect of validation and invaildation on positive and negative affectives experiences', *The Journal of Positive Psychology*, 2020.

'Ira Glass on Storytelling', *This American Life*, viewed 23 July 2021, <youtube.com/watch?v=X2wLP0izeJE>.

Jeremy E Sherman, 'We Are All Mojo Addicts', *Psychology Today*, 21 March 2017, <psychologytoday.com/au/blog/ambigamy/201703/we-are-all-mojo-addicts>.

Julie Beck, 'Study: Fight Performance Anxiety by Getting Excited', *The Atlantic*, 9 January 2014, <theatlantic.com/health/archive/2014/01/study-fight-performance-anxiety-by-getting-excited/282886>.

Leonard S Newman, Kimberley J Duff & Roy F Baumeister, 'A new
look at defensive projection: Thought suppression, accessibility, and
biased person perception', *Journal of Personality and Social
Psychology*, vol. 72, no. 5, 1997, pp. 980–1001.

Liz Mineo, 'Good genes are nice, but joy is better', *The Harvard
Gazette*, 11 April 2017, <news.harvard.edu/gazette/story/2017/04/
over-nearly-80-years-harvard-study-has-been-showing-how-to-
live-a-healthy-and-happy-life/>.

Manoj Thomas & Claire I Tsai, 'Psychological Distance and Subjective
Experience: How Distancing Reduces the Feeling of Difficulty',
Journal of Consumer Research, vol. 39, no. 2, 1 August 2012,
pp. 324–340.

Mark S Granovetter, 'The Strength of Weak Ties', *American Journal
of Sociology*, vol. 78, no. 6, 1973, pp. 1360–1380.

Marshall B Rosenberg, *Nonviolent Communication: A Language of Life*,
PuddleDancer Press, 2003.

Matthew A Killingsworth & Daniel T Gilbert, 'A Wandering Mind
Is an Unhappy Mind', *Science*, vol. 330, no. 6006, 2010, p. 932.

Nedra Glover Tawwab, *Set Boundaries, Find Peace: A Guide to
Reclaiming Yourself*, TarcherPerigee, 2021.

Phyllis Korkki, 'Need Motivation? Declare a Deadline', *The New York
Times*, 20 April 2013, <nytimes.com/2013/04/21/jobs/deadline-
pressure-the-great-motivator.html>.

R R Wing & R W Jeffery, 'Benefits of recruiting participants with
friends and increasing social support for weight loss and
maintenance', *Journal of Consulting and Clinical Psychology*, vol. 67,
no. 1, 1999, pp. 132–138.

Rachel Service, *How to break up with your Public Identity*,
TEDxMacquarieUniversity, September 2019, <ted.com/talks/
rachel_service_how_to_break_up_with_your_public_identity>.

Sandra Blakeslee, 'Cells That Read Minds', *The New York Times*,
10 January 2006, <nytimes.com/2006/01/10/science/cells-that-
read-minds.html>.

Sarah Gardner & Dave Albee, 'Study focuses on strategies for achieving goals, resolutions', *Press Releases*, 266, 2015, <scholar.dominican.edu/news-releases/266>.

Serena Chen, 'Give Yourself a Break: The Power of Self-Compassion', *Harvard Business Review*, September–October 2018, <hbr.org/2018/09/give-yourself-a-break-the-power-of-self-compassion>.

Teju Ravilochan, 'Could the Blackfoot Wisdom that Inspired Maslow Guide Us Now?', *GatherFor:*, 5 April 2021, <gatherfor.medium.com/maslow-got-it-wrong-ae45d6217a8c>.

Teresa M Amabile & Steven J Kramer, 'The Power of Small Wins', *Harvard Business Review*, May 2011, <hbr.org/2011/05/the-power-of-small-wins>.

'The Learning Zone Model', ThemPra Social Pedagogy, viewed 23 July 2021, <thempra.org.uk/social-pedagogy/key-concepts-in-social-pedagogy/the-learning-zone-model>.

Thomas A Harris, *I'm OK, You're OK: A Practical Guide to Transactional Analysis*, Harper & Row, 1967.

'Why You Should Put Yourself First', *Oprah's Lifeclass*, Oprah Winfrey Network, uploaded 29 March 2012, <youtube.com/watch?v=ZhqokZF5OFU>.

RESOURCES: MENTAL HEALTH SERVICE PROVIDERS

Listed below are mental health providers in Australia and New Zealand who can support you as you work through the steps of this book.

For support outside of Australia and New Zealand, please contact your national health service.

Some workplaces may also have an Employee Assistance Program, designed to enhance the emotional, mental and general psychological wellbeing of employees, and may include services for immediate family members. Reach out to your employer for further information.

Australia

A coach can be a great support through this period of change.

- NewAccess is a free coaching program designed to provide accessible, quality services for anyone finding it hard to manage life stress. The program aims to help people break the cycle of negative or unhelpful thoughts. <beyondblue.org.au/get-support/newaccess/about-newaccess>

- NewAccess is also available for any small business owner feeling stressed or overwhelmed about everyday challenges. Across six free sessions, you will be guided by a coach with a small business background who is specifically trained to provide a practical approach to problem-solving. <beyondblue.org.au/get-support/newaccess/newaccess-for-small-business-owners>

If you're searching for mental health support or counselling, try talking to your doctor first. They can assess you, and can refer you to another health professional if needed.

Otherwise, national support agencies include the following:

- Beyond Blue provides information and support to help everyone in Australia achieve their best possible mental health. <beyondblue.org.au> 1300 224 636

- Embrace Multicultural Mental Health gives multicultural communities access to resources, services and information in a culturally accessible format. <embracementalhealth.org.au> multicultural@mhaustralia.org (02) 6285 3100

- Lifeline Australia provides support if you are experiencing a personal crisis or have suicidal thoughts. You can call them 24 hours a day, seven days a week, from anywhere in Australia. <lifeline.org.au> 24-hour crisis line: 131 114

New Zealand

If you're searching for mental health support or counselling, try talking to your doctor first. They can assess you, and can refer you to another health professional if needed.

Otherwise, national helplines include the following:

- 1737 provides support if you're feeling stressed, down or a bit overwhelmed, or just need someone to talk to. Free call or text any time to talk to (or text with) a trained counsellor or peer support worker. <1737.org.nz> 1737

- Lifeline Aotearoa helpline and textline provides 24/7, confidential support from qualified counsellors and trained volunteers. lifeline.org.nz 0800 543 354 (0800 LIFELINE) or free text 4357 (HELP)

Mental Health Foundation of New Zealand also has a listing of community support groups, for free mental health support in your area. <mentalhealth.org.nz/groups>

www.ingramcontent.com/pod-product-compliance
Lightning Source LLC
Chambersburg PA
CBHW021140090426
42740CB00008B/861